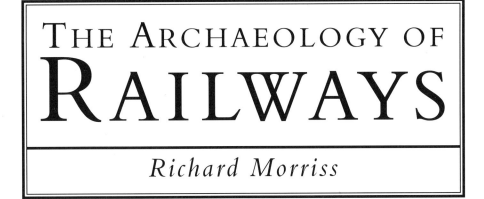

THE ARCHAEOLOGY OF
RAILWAYS

Richard Morriss

TEMPUS

First published 1999

PUBLISHED IN THE UNITED KINGDOM BY:

Tempus Publishing Ltd
The Mill, Brimscombe Port
Stroud, Gloucestershire GL5 2QG

PUBLISHED IN THE UNITED STATES OF AMERICA BY:

Tempus Publishing Inc.
2A Cumberland Street
Charleston, SC 29401

Tempus books are available in France, Germany and Belgium
from the following addresses:

Tempus Publishing Group	Tempus Publishing Group	Tempus Publishing Group
21 Avenue de la République	Gustav-Adolf-Straße 3	Place de L'Alma 4/5
37300 Joué-lès-Tours	99084 Erfurt	1200 Brussels
FRANCE	GERMANY	BELGIUM

British Library Cataloguing in Publication Data.
A catalogue record for this book is available from the British Library.

ISBN 0 7524 1430 5

Typesetting and origination by Tempus Publishing.
PRINTED AND BOUND IN GREAT BRITAIN.

Contents

List of illustrations

Note on the Illustrations

Unless otherwise stated the photographs in this book are by the author or from the author's collection. That collection has been built up over the years from photographs given by friends or those acquired from second hand and junk shops. Most are unidentified, though their locations can often be worked out. Others have a place and sometimes a date scribbled on the back. None of those used have any photographer's name on them and the author would like to apologise in advance in case of any inadvertent breach of copyright.

Cover illustration: A Type 47 diesel hauls a Shrewsbury-bound Inter-City train across the Belvidere Bridge over the River Severn in the early 1980s. The bridge, designed by William Baker and built by the Coalbrookdale Company in 1848-9, had just been restored.

Colour plates

Preface

'It is the peculiar privilege of the present generation
to live in the time of railways, the introduction of which,
rationally considered, must surely be esteemed one of the
greatest blessings ever conferred on the human race.'

Francis Whishaw, *Railways of Great Britain & Ireland* (1842)

Whilst those standing in a crowded late-running commuter train may dispute Whishaw's glowing acceptance of the railways, it is nevertheless true that the society in which we live was partly formed by them. Ten years before Whishaw wrote those lines it would have taken several days to get from London to Manchester; ten years after, it was possibly to get from one end of the country to the other in a day. Travel was also no longer the prerogative of the rich; the middle classes could afford it and, following the Acts of 1844 — which led to the statutory 'penny-a-mile' or 'Parliamentary' trains — and of 1883 — the 'Cheap Trains Act' — so could most of the working classes too.

Commuting led to the developments of the suburbs and satellite towns; longer distance travel led to a more united national outlook; and the need to properly timetable trains led to the end of local time in favour of new, standard, 'Railway Time'. These were some of the lesser effects, and the great economic benefits wrought by the development of an intensive national network of track is far less easy to quantify — as, indeed, are the environmental or social costs. Not everyone considered that the railways were a 'good thing' anyway. The eccentric but influential critic Ruskin thought that the 'hundred and fifty millions, with which we have paid men for digging ground from one place and depositing it in another' would have been better spent on beautiful new houses and churches rather than creating the 'very doubtful advantage of the power of going fast from place to place....The whole system of railroad travelling is addressed to people who, being in a hurry, are therefore, for the time being, miserable. ...The railroad...transmutes a man from a traveller into a living parcel.'

Britain's railways are still an important part of the country's transport infrastructure. They were exceptionally well-built and most of the stations, bridges, and earthworks in use today have been little altered since the second quarter of the nineteenth century. These historic structures are not museum pieces but integral parts of a modern network. Only on the abandoned lines do they take on the appearance of the antique and neglected, or the lovingly restored.

The archaeological resource of railways is immense — indeed, it is probably too immense. The richness of the resource has become a threat. It is taken by and large for granted, and it seems to be in little or no danger — but it is hard to believe now that in the 1960s there were plans to demolish architectural masterpieces like Bristol and Shrewsbury stations, and the far-famed Euston Arch was indeed lost. Since then matters have improved and the more important architectural features have been listed. Others, often little known or unrecognised, are still in danger of disappearing without record. Such structures are not always of any architectural merit or great historical interest, but they are or were part of a national network of railways whose impact cannot be underestimated and deserve at least to be recorded before they go. Many are worth more than that.

I: Introduction
1 Why Railway Archaeology?

Archaeology is still, in many people's eye, all about the digging up of the past. It is about people in an assortment of motley clothing kneeling down and scraping the earth with their trowels until some long-lost artefact is triumphantly rediscovered. Certainly excavation is an important part of the overall field of archaeology and, indeed, it can be used in railway archaeology to good effect, but it is only one part of a much wider subject.

At the risk of over simplification, archaeology is one of the two main strands of history. The other strand is that of documentary research, and the two have different approaches to achieve the same shared goal — a better understanding of the past. Documentary research relies on the objective study of primary and printed archive material whilst archaeology relies on the objective study of the physical remains. Neither can exist without the other; the documentary researcher has to make sure that the sequence of events evolving from that research is backed up by, and certainly not contradicted by, the physical evidence. Conversely, if the conclusions reached from the archaeological study of that evidence are not matched by the documentary research, they need to be reassessed. The main difference is that the evidence of the physical remains, if properly interpreted, should be more reliable than the documentary evidence — simply because buildings cannot make mistakes but a clerk of a few centuries ago could.

Railway archaeology is, therefore, one of the two branches of railway history and it can be a very wide subject. It does not begin with the Stephensons and the Stockton & Darlington Railway, but in the obscurity of the medieval period. The techniques involved vary from the traditional excavation of old waggonways to simple structural analysis — two very different disciplines. Whilst the use of archaeological techniques for the earlier railways may seem appropriate — especially when the surviving records are few and the routes are not shown on any maps — the use of the same techniques for railways in the steam age may not. After all, the railways created a massive amount of paperwork, legal, political, governmental, private, business and public. Hundreds, if not thousands, of books and tens of thousands of articles have been written, the results of millions of hours of research. What is there left to learn?

1   *A simple archaeological problem. The abutments of this former girder bridge carrying the PS&NWR over a road at Hanwood was clearly built in two phases. There is a vertical construction break between two slightly different sections of rough-cut masonry. The line was evidently doubled — but this did not quite fit with the written histories.*

The answer to that is — a surprising amount. Nine out of ten of the hundreds of books and articles on railways published every year are concerned with the locomotives that ran on them, varying in quality from repetitive collections of photographs of the 1950s to extraordinarily in-depth technical analyses of individual locomotives almost literally down to the last rivet. Of the other ten per cent, some will be on carriages and waggons, some on personal recollections, some on company histories, and some, a relatively tiny few, will deal with the architecture and civil engineering. It is in this last group that railway archaeology is the most relevant but, excepting a few notable exceptions, it is seldom applied.

Archaeological techniques do not have to be complex or expensive. Whilst the buried remains of a lost waggonway should be excavated with as much care as a prehistoric henge monument — especially given the fact that the timber trackwork will not always have lasted very well — such projects are very rare. The major excavation carried out in the Chatsworth Street cutting of the Liverpool & Manchester in the 1970s was very much the exception in studying the era of the steam railway and most railway archaeology is concerned instead with the study of buildings, structures, and earthworks.

This is usually non-destructive and, depending on the amount of information needed, can be quite simple. Railway buildings are not particularly complex. Most have been built in the past two centuries using construction techniques that are still familiar today. All that is needed is a good eye to distinguish the breaks between the various phases. Understanding the archaeology of a typical railway station involves little more than

*2   On parts of some main lines the archaeology of the past has been swept away by later changes.
         This view is of the former London & Birmingham Railway route in north London. Once there
         was only a double line of tracks to the south portal of the Primrose Hill tunnel, just visible in
         the distance. A second tunnel was opened in 1879 and then two more; the last major alterations
         were due to the introduction of suburban electric services in 1922.*

looking out for obvious changes in the materials being used in various parts of it — from
stone to brick, for example, or different types of brick — and changes in architectural
styles and detailing. There will be obvious or subtle breaks — construction breaks —
between them, usually vertical but sometimes horizontal. Similarly it should not be
difficult to see if windows and doorways have been blocked, or if windows and doorways
have been inserted. Changing buildings in this way would not be carried out on a whim
and there must have been a reason for spending the time and money on alterations. These
reasons should then be identified by looking at the way in which the internal spaces have
been altered, for example; have there been walls added or removed, or changes made to
the use of individual rooms or the entire station?

Similar questions can be asked when studying other railway buildings — the
locomotive sheds, goods sheds and signal boxes. Bridges can also be looked at with
something more than a purely aesthetic or engineering eye, as can the track formation
itself. The surviving earthworks of lost railway lines are usually easy to distinguish because
their form is quite unlike that of a road or of most abandoned canals. Providing that the
observations are objective, the archaeological process can be very simple and very useful.
Nevertheless, it is surprising sometimes how often it is ignored.

A basic example concerns the ill-fated Potteries, Shrewsbury & North Wales Railway,
which was later reopened as the better known Shropshire & Montgomeryshire Light

3   *Sometimes railway sites have been completely redeveloped. Margate, Kent, was served by two competing companies, the South Eastern and the London, Chatham & Dover railways, both of which had stations in the town. The SER station was on the seafront, and, to compete, the LC&DR built a second station alongside it — but it was never used. Both lie under the amusement park and few traces survived when this photograph was taken in 1979.*

Railway. Although originally planned as a humble mineral railway, its ambitions changed. The proprietors planned it to link the English Midlands with a proposed new port for the Irish traffic on the Lleyn peninsular and the Shrewsbury to Llanymynech section opened as a double-tracked passenger line in August 1866. It had closed by the end of the year, and, two years later reopened as a single line surviving until 1880.

Virtually all of the surviving track bed and bridges are for a double-track line. That was fairly standard, in England at least, even for lines that originally opened as single lines; the additional costs of building were considered to be slight and the hope was that traffic would require a second track sooner or later. However, on the PS&NWR line, the surviving single stone-built abutment of the former girder bridge at Hanwood, just outside Shrewsbury, was clearly of two separate phases with an obvious vertical construction break between the two. The only possible interpretation was that, at this point at least, the bridge was built only for a single line of railway which had subsequently been doubled. As all the other abutments on the line were of one build, it would seem that work on the single-tracked mineral line had started at the Shrewsbury end before the ambitions of the company changed, the partially completed section was doubled, and the rest was built double from the start. The simple archaeological evidence, from just one construction break, prompted further documentary research which confirmed this sequence of events. It is not a complex story, but one that had not been picked up in the existing published works on the line.

Detailed archaeological studies of railway buildings in the past few years, one of the first being the Royal Commission on Historical Monuments survey of the original York terminus published as part of their wider inventory of York in 1972, almost invariable add to our understanding of them but have been small in number. Certainly there have been studies by specialist and often very skilled enthusiasts but these have often been biased more towards the railway functions than to a more holistic approach that includes changes in structural techniques and architectural style.

There remain, up and down Britain, thousands of railway related buildings and hundreds of miles of abandoned lines that have never been studied by even the most basic archaeological approach. A recent study of the main transport corridor through Wolverhampton showed up several intriguing railway structures and buildings that had previously been virtually ignored and certainly not properly studied, including a goods transhipment shed of 1848 that had hardly ever been used for its original purposes; a surviving cast-iron girder bridge of the same year fossilised within later alterations, and a small and as yet unexplained brick structure that looks suspiciously like a very early engine shed.

The fate of the railway heritage of Wolverhampton is similar to that of other towns of similar size — a mixture of good and bad. Its two main line stations were built side by side to similar Italianate designs; the High Level of 1848 was bulldozed as part of the electrification of the West Coast main line and replaced by a modern one in the 1960s, leaving only a subway and linking colonnade to the Low Level station. That had closed to passengers and been converted into a goods station but in the late 1980s there were plans for a railway heritage centre. These came to nothing and the station is about to be redeveloped, though as the buildings are listed they will at least be retained. On the plus side, the former detached two-storey entrance block to the High Level station, a smaller local attempt to match the famous Euston Arch, has, after many years of dereliction, been restored. The local authority is fortunately aware of its railway heritage and is trying to do all it can in the planning system to protect it; this, sadly, is not always the case.

The steady process of demolition of old railway buildings, which reached a peak in the 1960s and '70s, has slowed down but still continues. This is another reason for the importance of railway archaeology. Obviously not all buildings or structures can or should be retained simply because they are old. Fossilising the past is in no one's interest and the financial cost of doing so would be far too high anyway. Judgements have to be made as to what should be retained and what should go and those judgements can only be made properly on the basis of knowing their relative merits. That information can only be gained by objective study, combining the skills of the archaeologist and the documentary researcher.

Of course, the information gleaned by an archaeological study of any building is no good unless it is in a presentable form. There are several levels of reporting on a building, ranging from a brief written description to an illustrated monograph, but the important thing is to get that information across in a suitable and meaningful way. Even the most basic description should be accompanied by a photograph, and drawings — even if they vary from little more than a sketch to a properly scaled brick-by-brick plot — help enormously. Drawing also helps in the analysis, and, if annotated properly, in presenting the relevant information. As a last resort, a drawing or a photograph will at least provide a permanent record of a building about to be demolished.

4   *Archaeology, particularly in railways, is not concerned with just the antique. Accelerating technological changes and the often odd decisions made by the powers that be can lead to short lives for modern equipment. The Woodhead cross-Pennine route was electrified in the early 1950s and a costly new tunnel was built. By 1980 the line had closed and within a few years all the expensive installations were scrapped.*

This book is not about archaeological techniques or philosophy; it is simply an attempt to explain the developments of the various elements of the railway system that may be the subject of archaeological research — the earthworks, track and buildings, in other words, the engineering and the architecture. It is not about the rolling stock that made use of the engineering and this was a deliberate decision. Locomotives and rolling stock have been more than well covered in the existing railway literature and little can be added — and certainly not by a non-specialist. To have included them in the confines of this book would have restricted the space available for the rest.

This is not to say that locomotives and rolling stock do not have their own archaeological conundrums. After all, little except the chassis and wheels of most of the steam locomotives majestically gleaming in their period splendour on our preserved railway survive from when they were first built. Boilers, cylinders and fireboxes all had to be replaced on a regular basis, and most of these locomotives were rescued from scrap yards where many of their other fittings went missing. Railway companies also had a quite sensible habit of interchanging parts between locomotives of the same class.

Carriages also can have a story. In the late 1980s members of the Llangollen Railway Society found the body of an old railway carriage near Dorrington, Shropshire. The owner gave it to them and told them of a tradition that it had been in a crash on the nearby Shrewsbury & Hereford Railway in 1870. Close study of the vehicle showed it to be a typical First Class carriage of the 1850s, but one that had been changed obviously before being taken off its chassis. Internal compartments had been removed and wire mesh put on at least one of the windows. It appeared to have been converted into a van of some sort. With this information in mind, the documentary research managed to find out that this had been an original coach of the Shrewsbury & Hereford that had been converted into the mess van of a breakdown train which had crashed en route to a minor accident in 1873.

With locomotives and carriages, simply looking at and recording the changes made to them over the years will be useless without a basic grasp of the mechanical engineering involved. With the rest of the railway heritage, the same rule applies, only it is a basic understanding of the civil engineering, architectural, and structural techniques, and of the use of buildings and structures, that is needed instead. These are the subjects of this book.

2 Outline history

By the time the Liverpool & Manchester Railway opened in 1830, there had already been railways in Britain for well over 200 years. Passengers had been officially carried on railway trains for nearly a quarter of a century and steam power had been in railway use for even longer. Nevertheless, the Liverpool & Manchester Railway, whilst not the beginning of railway history, was one of its most important landmarks. It represented the first modern railway — a railway formed by a public company with its proposals ratified by Parliament, its line engineered to the most exacting standards of the day, and most of its traffic hauled by locomotive power.

To briefly outline the developments of the things that made the opening of the Liverpool & Manchester possible it is necessary to step back to the start of the seventeenth century. Claims have been made, quite convincingly, that railways of sorts must have existed in the ancient world, even if they were just temporary track or sled runs used for construction purposes. Proto-railways in the mines of Middle Europe have been identified in the writings and illustrations of Sebastian Münster in his *Cosmographia Universalis* of 1550 and, more famously, in Agricola's *De Re Metallica* of 1556.

These were primitive underground railways in the mines. A small four-wheeled waggon known as a *hund* ran on two parallel planks; underneath the *hund* was a projecting iron guide-pin which fitted into the narrow gap between the two planks and thus kept the waggon from derailing. In the later sixteenth century, Queen Elizabeth, acutely aware of Britain's relative backwardness in mining, actively encouraged foreign experts to settle and work in the country. It was probably copper miners from the Tirol, in what is now modern Austria, that first introduced the *hund* to England. They were employed by the new Company of Mines Royal when they settled near Derwentwater, Cumbria, in the 1560s. However, the mines were singularly unsuccessful and the *hund* had little effect on railway development in this country — but there is as yet no conclusive evidence of anything that we would identify as a 'railed way' in Britain until the very end of the sixteenth century. Ironically, it will inevitably be in these long-abandoned mines that future railway archaeologists eventually find the evidence for our railway prehistory.

At that time the roads were poor, and had been since the departure of the Roman legions. Mostly unmetalled tracks, they were either quagmires in the wet months or rutted and rock hard in the dry ones. Uncomfortable for pedestrian or rider, they were virtually impossible for the heavy lumbering wagons needed for the transport of heavy goods. What little industrial traffic that did exist was mostly carried by pack horse. The end of the sixteenth century, however, was also the time when coal was becoming an important commodity and coal mines were being opened up in many areas of the country. The problem then was to get the coal to the markets.

5   *A contemporary engraving of 1788 on surveys by John Gibson showing a steeply graded double-track waggonway in action in Tyneside. The large horse-drawn wagons are taking coal to a riverside wharf. On the right a full wagon is being braked by the seated driver whilst the horse trots behind; the empty wagon is being hauled by the horse up the slope.*

The most reliable form of transport was by water. Indeed, the manner whereby most coal went to London gave it its earliest name — *sea coal*. The colliery owners had to find a way of getting the coal to the quays. Providing the mines were close to a navigable river, this was not a great problem. Even in the heart of England, coal mines in east Shropshire were able to send their product away on the River Severn, one of the most important navigable highways in Europe.

The increasing demand for coal eventually led to the exhaustion of those mines nearest to the sea or the rivers and this in turn led to a need to provide an economical method of bridging the ever increasing gap between the wharves and the newer collieries. Using men or packhorses on the primitive road systems just added to the cost of the coal and new methods were needed.

Almost simultaneously two wooden railways — or waggonways — appear in the annals, the first in Nottinghamshire, the second in Shropshire. Whilst these are documented, it is of course possible and perhaps almost inevitable that there were others in existence at the same time. The first recorded *Rayle-way* was built by a colliery owner, Huntingdon Beaumont, in 1603-4 from Wollaton (just outside Nottingham) to the Trent and is thought to be about two miles long. Little else is known about it. Fortunately, there are

6   *Restored plateway trucks on plateway tracks at the Blists Hill part of the Ironbridge Gorge Museum, Shropshire in 1982. Trucks such as this continued in use up until the 1950s on some internal plateways in some works in the area.*

more details about the second. In 1605 two men, Richard Wilcox and William Wells, leased two parcels of land in Broseley from the Lord of the Manor, James Clifford. One plot contained a coal pit, the other, a wharf on the River Severn. The land in between the two belonged to Clifford and in that year the two men applied for a right-of-way — or *wayleave* — over it. That in itself was a common enough practise but they also applied to the local government body of that region — then still the Council of the Welsh Marches — to build a 'very artificial Engine or Instrumente of Timber' over Clifford's land to link their pit and their wharf. This 'Engine' consisted of 'fframes and Rayles' on which small wagons could run — in effect, a railway.

The fact that the two men went to so much trouble to get permission from the authorities suggests that they were unsure of their rights with such a novel form of transportation. Within a year they were back at the Council complaining that Clifford, jealous of their success, had ordered 'a nomber of lewd persons, being the scummes and dregges of many countries...[to]...hack hewe and displace' their railway not just once, but again after the ravages of the first attack had been repaired for the then not inconsiderable sum of £20. Clifford replied by claiming that the 'Engine' had been too expensive to run and that Wilcox and Wells had sabotaged it in a Jacobean insurance fiddle. The outcome of the case is not known as the papers are lost, but within a few years Clifford had built several such railways himself, including one that consisted of 'Rayles from the wharf places by the River of Severne unto the face of the wall of the Coles', and was claiming in turn that Wilcox and Wells had attacked them. The railway era had started — along with the truculence and bitterness that would surround it for over three centuries and later divert money from the shareholders' pockets into those of the lawyers.

Their initial success is difficult to assess. Certainly by lifting the wagon wheels from the mud and spreading their loads along parallel timber balks the costs of hauling coals would have been greatly reduced. Creating even gradients on routes that were mostly down to the river quays would have improved matters further still. At first quite primitive, these early railways soon developed into something a little more sophisticated. Even by 1608 Clifford's railways had 'tilting Rayles', suggesting something more than paired wooden balks of timber on at least part of the line.

These railway became known by different names in different parts of the country — *railways, railroads, woodenways* and *waggonways*. In the north-east they were sometimes called *Newcastle Roads* and it was in that part of the country that they expanded the most as the demand for *sea coal* grew. These include one built over Ryton Moor in County Durham before 1663 of which some traces still remain and, more famously, the Tanfield Wagonway, built in the 1720s to a standard probably unsurpassed in its day. Unlike most other lines, this crossed a watershed and did not compromise on engineering. It has left the remarkable legacy of the Causey Arch and, less remarkable but just as historically important, the Beckley Burn embankment. Shortly after that line was built, Ralph Allen built one from his quarries at Combe Down through his Prior Park estate to the wharves on the Avon in Bath, an early example of a waggonway not dedicated to the transport of coal.

All of these lines were built by individuals, companies, or perhaps groups of companies to serve specific needs and were mostly built on private land that they owned or they had amicable agreements with the owners. The Middleton Railway represents another railway landmark, for in 1758 its promoters had to obtain an Act of Parliament to affirm wayleaves along its route, a process that would become very important in the following century.

The eighteenth century saw several important innovations on the waggonways. By 1729 the Coalbrookdale Company in Shropshire were making cast-iron wheels for the wagons, and later introduced iron axles. These increased the weight of the wagons and also the wear and tear on the wooden rails and it was also the Coalbrookdale Company that can claim to have introduced the first iron rails by 1767 to compensate. Civil engineering also improved, especially in the later eighteenth century. This coincided with the development of the canal system. Waggonways were seen as logical feeder lines to the canals in places where it would be too expensive to build a branch canal, and many railway lines were built by the canal companies.

These more ambitious lines benefited from the lessons learnt by the canal builders. Canals, by their very nature, required a much greater accuracy in their construction than the railways. It was vital to fill the cuts with adequate supplies of virtually still water for navigation, and that expensively garnered water was not to be wasted. As a result, the lines of the canals had to be carefully surveyed to avoid too many locks. The earlier canals tended to do this by keeping to the natural contours of the land, though later ones were more ambitious. Even so, men like Brindley, Jessop and Telford had to develop the techniques and, more importantly, the confidence to build tunnels several miles long through the most difficult rock strata and soaring aqueducts over the deepest valleys.

The lines connected with the canals were also different than the older ones in that they were generally public and no longer just dedicated to coal; they could take virtually the same type of traffic carried on the canals. A by-product of this was a very early form of containerism, where large containers were shipped from waggonway to barge — though this system was never a great success or particularly popular. Such canal-supported or owned lines also tended to be much longer than the coal lines and occurred in parts of the country well away from the coalfields.

In 1801 the Surrey Iron Railway obtained its Act and two years later, double tracked throughout, opened between Croydon and the banks of the Thames in Wandsworth nearly nine miles away. Engineered by William Jessop, this was the first railway to be promoted by a separate company in order to make profits from public trade. Others followed, but there was no great surge in the number of the new public railways. Amongst the more significant was the Oystermouth line authorised in 1804 and opened in 1807; this was the first commercial railway to carry fare-paying passengers.

By the first decade of the nineteenth century most of the elements of a modern railway were established. Civil engineering was capable of carrying the lines over almost any difficult terrain; wooden track was gradually being replaced by iron; a legal framework had been established; and lines were being promoted by independent companies. Schemes were being put forward by people thinking about a national network of railways; amongst them were Benjamin Outram, the main promoter of plateways who as early as 1799 thought that 'it is exceedingly probable that Railways will soon become general for the transport of Merchandize thro' the commercial parts of this Kingdom....'. In 1800 William Thomas of Northumberland suggested a network of plateways that could take ordinary road vehicles and in the following year James Anderson called for a public network of plateways on a similar system. William James was another pioneer, writing in 1808, and he actually built the horse-drawn Stratford & Moreton Tramway (opened in 1826) as part of his grand scheme to link London and Birmingham. He was later involved in the early years of the Liverpool & Manchester Railway.

None of these schemes were met with any great enthusiasm. Although the waggonways and plateways did serve a very useful, and in some cases, vital transport role, that role was purely a local one. For longer distances, the canal and river systems or coastal shipping were far more efficient and cheaper, and even some of the main roads had been upgraded to reasonable standards by virtue of the turnpike system. A national railway system could only work if it could be quicker and more efficient than existing modes of transport. Gravity and the horse were simply not up to the task, and attempts to use sail power — firstly by Sir Humphrey Mackworth on a line at Neath in 1698 and later on the Oystermouth Railway in 1807 — were interesting experiments but not serious possibilities. It was only the development of the steam locomotive that made the modern railway possible.

Steam power has an ancient history. Hero of Alexandria had already invented the steam turbine — as a toy — in Egypt around the time of Cleopatra but nothing serious was to

7   *A modern Liverpool-bound DMU approaches Rainhill station on the former Liverpool &*
Manchester Railway, scene of the famous Trials of 1829 that finally demonstrated the triumph
of the steam locomotive over the stationary engine or horse.

be done with the power of steam until the late seventeenth century. Early in the eighteenth, Thomas Newcomen developed the first successful steam engine for pumping mines and this was improved upon by John Smeaton, James Watt and others later in the century. These were all stationary steam engines, although it was possible to use them for railway purposes by hauling trains by way of ropes. This was first used on inclined planes on the Shropshire Canal in 1791, on which cradles carried small tub-boats between levels of canal. The first steam powered incline to be specifically built for a railway was near Preston in 1803 on a line linking the two sections of the Lancaster Canal.

Until the start of the 1840s, rope-haulage of trains by stationary steam engines remained one of the options open to railway engineers and many lines were deliberately built with fairly long level sections linked by steep steam-powered inclines. These so-called 'hybrid' railways were seriously seen as the only way of building new lines. When the Liverpool & Manchester Railway was being built there were still plans to make it rope-hauled throughout, and locomotive power only became properly established at the Rainhill trials held in 1829.

The Frenchman Nicholas Cugnot had developed a steam powered gun transporter in 1770 and in Britain William Murdoch had invented a small road-going steam carriage in the 1780s. Both men were dissuaded from taking their ideas any further and it was not until the very start of the nineteenth century that the first self-propelled steam railway locomotive was built. Richard Trevithick built a small locomotive for the plateways at

8   *A new electric multiple unit heads towards Deptford station on the original four-mile long brick viaduct of the London & Greenwich Railway, the first steam-hauled line in the capital. The section from London to Deptford opened in 1836.*

Coalbrookdale in 1802 but the experiment was for some reason abandoned. In 1804 a similar engine was tried, more successfully, on a plateway at Pen-y-Darren in South Wales. It was ahead of its time, because although it hauled wagons successfully it also broke the cast iron rails regularly. In 1808 Trevithick had another locomotive built in Bridgnorth, by the Hazeldine & Raistrick and called it *Catch-me-who-can*. A circular plateway track was set up in Euston, then on the outskirts of London, and the locomotive ran around it hauling a carriage behind. Braver members of the public could pay to ride in the carriage — and it can thus lay claim to be the world's first steam passenger train. Unfortunately the rails again proved to be the problem and kept breaking; with public interest dwindling the enterprise was closed.

In 1812 a new type of locomotive was built by Matthew Murray and John Blenkinsop for the Middleton Colliery. One line of the rails were changed to a cast-iron continuous rack and the crankshaft on the locomotive worked a pinion that meshed with the rack; the locomotive was a success and two others were built; a handful of other lines were built using this system but all were soon displaced by later improvements although the Middleton line retained its rack system until 1835.

Other locomotives evolved, built by men like William Hedley and Timothy Hackworth, and then George Stephenson. His first locomotive was the *Blücher*, built in 1814-15, but by the time he had built the *Locomotion* in 1825 for use on the Stockton & Darlington Railway the performance had improved considerably. The Stockton & Darlington line was

9   *Philip Hardwick's famous 'Euston Arch' at the southern end of the London & Birmingham Railway fell victim to modernisation in the early 1960s but the fine Ionic centrepiece of his contemporary Birmingham station, later known as Curzon Street, survives — largely because it was downgraded to a goods depot as early as 1854. The original hotel and iron trainsheds have long gone, but the main block has recently been restored.*

a typical hybrid line, with some sections powered by stationary steam engines, some by horse, and some by steam locomotives. Passengers were initially hauled in a horse-drawn carriage. The main difference between this and earlier public lines was that the locomotive haulage was frequent — and relatively reliable.

The locomotive had yet to prove itself, nevertheless. The next two Stephenson lines, the Liverpool & Manchester and the Canterbury & Whitstable were engineered in such a way to make either locomotive or stationary steam engines possible. The Canterbury & Whitstable was the first to open, in the summer of 1830, and could claim to have the first regular passenger trains hauled by steam locomotive. Most of the line, however, was on inclines powered by stationary engines, and the locomotive — Stephenson's *Invicta* — was not a success. By the end of the 1830s the level sections were being temporarily worked by horses.

The Rainhill Trials of 1829 demonstrated the improvements made to locomotives by that time and it was decided that the Liverpool & Manchester main line would be worked by locomotives for both passenger and goods traffic. Once they were found to be successful, the modern railway was born. Even so, it should be remembered that not all the line was locomotive hauled in 1830; the two end sections in Liverpool to the passenger and goods terminals were worked by stationary engines down relatively steep inclines. The line was also something of an engineering triumph, showing in its earthworks and bridges the ambition of the new age.

Up until this point virtually all railways had been built for goods traffic, and still, particularly for coal traffic. Passenger traffic was seldom considered, though no doubt since the seventeenth century the odd lift had been 'cadged' by workers and others on a passing waggonway wagon. The remarkable feature of the Liverpool & Manchester was the amount of people who wanted to use it — so many, in fact, that after the line opened goods traffic was not started until additional locomotives were available as all the others were hauling passenger trains. The passenger trade then became an important part of the railway system and led to the creation of huge impressive stations and hotels in the major towns and hundreds of other stations of varying architectural quality throughout the country.

This mass mobilisation of people was not welcomed by many of the opponents of the railways. Whilst some of these were simply vested interests threatened by the 'new' form of transport — such as the canals and the turnpikes — others were more concerned with matters that seem completely irrelevant today. The Duke of Wellington is said to have disapproved because they made the working class more mobile, and John Ruskin saw railways creating the 'very doubtful advantage of the power of going fast from place to place'.

In the 1830s the basic infrastructure of the railway network was begun. The construction of these new railways could be extraordinarily expensive but they again benefited from the earlier experiences of the canal builders. When the larger canals were being built the capital that needed to be raised was enormous but potential investors were easy to convince. The canal companies had created a financial system capable of raising the huge funds needed to build them. The genuine financial successes of the major canals led to tens of thousands of others being desperate to invest in, and to profit by, the seemingly infallible new form of transport. In the resulting 'Canal Mania' by no means all of the schemes were worth investing in, but this did not stem the flow of private money into these public companies. Despite the huge losses inevitably made by large numbers of these investors, the same thing would happen again in the railway age — not once, but in several 'Railways Manias' of varying intensity.

After a brief spasm in the mid-1820s the first real mania began in 1835 and lasted for a couple of years. The 1840s saw a rapid expansion in the railway network. As more and more lines were built and more and more towns became connected to what Ruskin called 'the iron veins of England' (and of the rest of Britain, of course), investors seemed to become desperate not to miss out on the apparently easy profits available. Gradually the lines planned became less and less sensible but the money continued to pour in. Several lines were promoted by less-than-scrupulous companies that had no real confidence in them ever succeeding economically, and no doubt there were some that were completely fraudulent. The economic feeding frenzy peaked between 1844 and 1847 — and then the bubble burst. Even the greatest entrepreneur of all, George Hudson, the 'Railway King', lost virtually everything in 1849. Several lines were delayed, such as the Shrewsbury & Hereford Railway; two out of five lines authorised by Parliament were never built; and a few, including the London, Brighton & South Coast Railway's Uckfield branch, were never finished.

10   *Despite the ruling of the Gauge Commission, Brunel's Broad Gauge continued in use on the Great Western Railway's main line until 1892. The supposed superior speed and power of Broad Gauge locomotives was never proven. This is* Iron Duke, *a GWR 4-2-2 express passenger engine built at Swindon in 1847, the first of the famous* Lord of the Isles *class.*

One of the best monuments to the Mania was built for Hudson's York & North Midland Railway. Anxious about the competition, the company decided to cut the route miles of their line between York and Leeds by building a new cut-off line from Copmanthorpe on the main line to Tadcaster on a branch then under construction. Authorised in 1845 work was well under way by 1849 and a very fine masonry viaduct had been finished taking the line over the River Wharfe on the outskirts of Tadcaster. Following Hudson's collapse, the enterprise was abandoned and the viaduct unused for nearly 40 years until a long siding from Tadcaster station was laid to serve a mill on the opposite side of the river. This very expensively constructed siding was little used and was lifted at the end of the 1950s. The local town council have now made the trackbed and viaduct an attractive footpath.

Apart from a brief revival in 1852, the 1850s saw a dramatic fall in the number of new proposals and a steady consolidation of the system. Confidence returned gradually and by the start of the 1860s there was another large rise in the number of schemes. This time the numbers of new lines being promoted may not have been as great as in the 1840s, but their chances of economic success were generally quite poor. Railways were built to serve large areas of sparsely populated mid-Wales for example, and others were wildly ambitious. The Potteries, Shrewsbury & North Wales Railway was originally promoted as a short mineral line but, caught up in the excitement, ended up projecting a new direct route from Stoke-on-Trent through Shrewsbury and the Welsh mountains to carry the

11   A classic scene of the steam railway period. A L&NER Pullman train hauled by a B1 class 4-6-0 leaves Newcastle-on-Tyne sometime in the 1930s. The fine triple-span curving trainshed, designed by John Dobson and Robert Stephenson, was one of the first of its kind when finished in 1850 and survives. Most of the working paraphernalia of signals and signs has been replaced, especially since the East Coast main line was recently electrified.

Irish traffic to a new port at Porthdinlleyn. In the end the company spent nearly two million pounds, most of it on legal fees, in building a little-used line between Shrewsbury and Llanymynech, on the Welsh border. Nevertheless, the surviving track bed of this eccentric railway shows that it was designed for main line standards, with few sharp curves or steep gradients.

By this time the steam railway in Britain had become predictable and reliable. Equally importantly, standardisation of gauge, timetabling, fares and even time, had helped the railways weld the country together in a way that had never been done before. The question of gauge had been settled by Parliament by the passing of the Gauge Act in 1846. Up until then the two main rival gauges, Stephenson's original 4ft $8\frac{1}{2}$in 'narrow gauge' and Brunel's more ambitious Great Western Railway 7ft $0\frac{1}{4}$in 'Broad gauge' had been used. The increasing rail mileage had led to increasing numbers of places where the two main gauges had met, and where everything from passengers to freight had to be transferred from the one gauge to the other. This led to delays, increased costs, opportunities for thefts, and for breakages. The Gauge Act followed on from a report by a commission set up to look into the matter, which came down in favour of the 'narrow' gauge. New Broad Gauge routes were discouraged, though not actually forbidden, but it was a victory for what now became the official 'Standard' gauge; the Great Western stubbornly continued with their 'Seven foot' until 1892.

12   *The use of diesels for main line traffic was quite late in Britain, and not established until the late 1950s. The most powerful diesel locomotives in the world were, for a time, the 'Deltics' used on the East Coast line. In January 1978 No.55 015* Tulyar *is seen at London King's Cross about to haul an Aberdeen express; the locomotive has since been preserved.*

The main changes to the railways were confined to improvements in the track and safety issues and, more importantly, to locomotives and rolling stock. Engines became larger and more powerful, and carriages became larger and more comfortable; in real terms, fares continually dropped leading to a steady rise in passenger figures. Goods traffic benefited from the generally buoyant economy of the nineteenth century.

Apart from the main line railway system, there were also many hundreds of industrial railways of all sorts, ranging in size from small narrow gauge factory lines to very large dock railways using standard gauge stock and having many miles of track. The basic construction methods for these railways tended to be of a more temporary nature than the public lines and the nature of some industries, especially extractive ones, meant that the rails were constantly being lifted and relaid. Some, however, were permanent features of the landscape for many years, if not for a century or more, and only finally succumbed to road traffic from the 1950s onwards. Such lines differed little from lesser rural public railways in their civil or mechanical engineering.

The least studied railways of all are probably those used underground in the collieries, which have the longest history of all beginning with the medieval *hunds* and ending in quite sophisticated and semi-automated electric railways used in pits until the massive closures of the 1980s and '90s. The last major underground industrial railway was the temporary narrow gauge system used in the construction of the Channel Tunnel.

13   *The use of electric traction came surprisingly early to the railways, and was sufficiently developed and reliable by the start of the twentieth century to persuade several companies to use it on heavily used sections of track, particularly for stopping trains. The Midland Railway introduced 6,600 volts AC electric multiple units on the Lancaster to Morecambe line in 1908 and one of the power coaches is seen nearing completion at Derby Works. It ran for over half a century.*

Private railways were also built for a variety of other uses, of which one of the most important was for the military. The larger ordnance depots, such as those at Longmoor and Donnington, were served by their own internal railway systems. Other lines were sometimes taken over to serve new munition or stores depots on their routes; in Shropshire, for example, after 1939 the Cleobury Mortimer & Ditton Priors Railway was taken over by the Royal Navy and the Shropshire & Montgomeryshire by the Army.

There was a late spurt of public railway building at the end of the nineteenth century. A series of recessions in agriculture from the 1880s onwards was one main reason. It was felt that rail access to the more remote areas would help, but the cost of building lines to normal standards would be uneconomic. In 1896 the Light Railways Act allowed such lines to be built under a Light Railway Order rather than an expensive private act, and by limiting the maximum speed of the trains, lighter track and earthworks could be used and there was no need for level crossings or complex signalling. Several of the new lines built under the act were to a narrow gauge, further cutting costs.

With the development of road transport in the early years of the twentieth century, railways first began to meet serious competition. As the railways had been built by competing companies and with no overall national plan, many lines were duplications and split the potential traffic revenues unnecessarily. This can be seen to extremes in some of the former coal mining valleys of South Wales where two or even three separate

14   Railways always seem to have a fascination for the British, which increased surprisingly with the end of main line steam in 1968. Even before then, antique engines had been restored to work 'specials' — such as this ex-Caledonian 4-2-2 No.123, built in 1886 and seen here at Dundee West in 1960. The locomotive survives but the fine ex-Caledonian station was demolished after closing in 1965.

companies vied for the same traffic. As late as 1899 the Great Central built another main line route from the north into London, a scheme that never had any chance of returning dividends to its investors. All this helped weaken their commercial fight against the lorry and the motor car.

By the end of the First World War even the larger companies were in financial difficulties and nationalisation of the railways was being discussed seriously — especially as, under direct Government control for the duration, their performance had been remarkably good considering the difficult conditions that they had to work under. Nationalisation had first been recommended in the 1840s but free trade was the buzzword of the nineteenth century and government control of the railways was considered to be an anathema. Despite political support for nationalisation after the war, the issue was fudged and instead of going ahead with full compulsory purchase of the system, nearly all the country's railways, well over a hundred of them, were amalgamated into four unequal 'groups' by an Act of 1922 that came into force at the start of the following year. The creation of the 'Big Four' — the London Midland & Scottish, the Great Western, the Southern, and the London & North Eastern, effectively created regional monopolies, although there was still a degree of inter-company competition left in the system.

The real competition was not from the other companies, but from road transport. As the number of private and commercial vehicles grew — along with the more adaptable

15   *Throughout the country there are now preserved railways attempting to recreate a past that
      probably never truly existed. Nevertheless, they help keep railway history alive. This is Haven
      Street, on the Isle of Wight Steam Railway. The locomotive, No.W24 Calbourne, is an 0-
      4-4T Adams Class 02 built for the London & South Western Railway in 1891 and rebuilt
      by the Southern Railway in 1925 for the island, remaining in service until 1967.*

motor bus — railways began to lose trade. To cope, new, cheaper and more frequently
unstaffed stations were built wherever possible and, by the 1930s, the 'Big Four' were
actively co-operating in several schemes to pool resources. The container system was tried
out in an effort to co-operate with the road hauliers as well and more and more
automation began to be applied to railway operation. To many people, the era of the 'Big
Four' is seen as the golden age of the railways, though this is probably more to do with
nostalgia than accurate reflection. It was, in any case, a short age because in 1939 the whole
network once again came under Government control for the Second World War and
although the companies were released afterwards, they were in no state to survive without
the nationalisation promised by the victorious post-war Labour government. Then, for
the first time there was, under the auspices of the new British Transport Commission, a
chance to have a truly integrated transport policy incorporating a nationally run railway
system. At the same time this could benefit from the new types of motive power being
developed.

   Up until nationalisation the steam locomotive and all the infrastructure that supported
it — engine sheds, water troughs, turntables, etc. — remained the prime motive force on
British Railways and would continue to do so until the start of the 1960s; in 1968 it ended.

As early as 1835 a model electric locomotive had been made by Thomas Davenport in the United States, and in 1842 Robert Davidson experimented with a five ton electric locomotive on the Edinburgh & Glasgow Railway. A public electric railway was opened in Germany in 1881 and the Volks' Electric Railway was opened on Brighton seafront in 1883.

Despite regionally successful electrification before the First World War around London, in the north-east of England and on the Morecambe-Lancaster route, wholehearted electric main line electrification did not occur in Britain until the Manchester-Wath line scheme (started before the Second World War but postponed because of it) was opened in 1954. Ironically, this line closed less than thirty years later. Further electrification, and all the associated paraphernalia of overhead wires, etc., has taken place since on many of the main line routes, though many others are still diesel hauled.

The first reasonably successful diesels on British railways were shunting locomotives introduced in the 1930s by the London Midland & Scottish Railway and the same company built the first successful main line diesel in 1947. It was not until the late 1950s that main line diesels began to replace steam engines for both passenger and goods traffic. The delays in whole-hearted electrification of the network led to the continuation of diesel traction in most parts of the country and many of the diesel locomotives in use are now well over 30 years old.

After nationalisation, the most dramatic and controversial event for the railways took place in the early 1960s with the publication of Richard Beeching's report on the *Reshaping of British Railways*. In it he recommended a radical overhaul of the whole system and wholesale closures of its loss-making branches and duplicate routes. It contained a great deal of sound economic sense but also what many considered to be a strong anti-rail bias. The lorry and the car had indeed eaten deeply into the revenue of the railways and keeping the less profitable rural services was seen as a huge drain on resources. Other factors — social and environmental — were largely ignored during a time when the great motorway building boom was just beginning and the idea of an integrated transport system had been abandoned.

The drastic cuts in the railways inevitably led to dramatic losses to a century or more of railway heritage. The track beds were usually sold off in indecent haste, leaving little chance for local authorities or individuals time to consider taking them over for other uses or for raising the necessary funds to do so. There was a fine opportunity to create a national network of cycle and footpaths, for example, that was never taken. The ironwork of most bridges was sold for scrap and gaps made in the routes as a result. Generally, track beds were sold to adjacent landowners, fragmenting the ownership of each line. Stations were either sold for conversion to private houses or, far worse, allowed to fall into ruin. Many other station and ancillary buildings were simply demolished and few records of their passing were made.

British Railways conservation record on their surviving lines was often little better. The demolition of the old Euston station, and especially of Hardwick's great portico, in the early 1960s was greeted with horror by most people — especially as the modern replacement was, at best, a convenient if architecturally indifferent building. Other fine stations were also threatened, including St Pancras in London, and some were fully or partially demolished, including the first station in York and the splendid Glasgow St Enoch's; many others became more and more run down because of poor maintenance and, after hundreds became unmanned as a cost-saving exercise, because of more unofficial vandalism.

There was an apparent change of policy in the 1970s but this was erratic; some good work on restoration was done but other decisions continued to surprise. Perhaps the most baffling was the demolition of most of the admittedly much-altered Derby station originally designed by Francis Thompson. Derby is a ancient county town but was also a pivotal rail centre since the Midland Railway made it their headquarters. The area around the station developed as a railway suburb and in it are the famous locomotive works, the roundhouse, several large warehouses, rows of workers' cottages restored at the start of the 1980s, Thompson's Midland Hotel of 1841 and the nearly contemporary Brunswick Inn. The station was the focal point of this remarkable collection of buildings — but all that was worthy was pulled down by British Rail, despite the protests of a wide range of amenity groups, in 1984.

At that time the railways again faced further decline and closures in the face of a government with a definite anti-rail and pro-road agenda. The vicious cuts recommended in the ill-thought out Serpel Report of 1983, however, proved far too extreme to be implemented. Instead, government policy turned to the privatisation of the railway system, not on a logical regional basis but on a peculiar tiered one that separated track, rolling stock and operator. It remains to be seen how this will work, but the standards of the railways have, in the 1990s, with a few exceptions, been very disappointing.

On the positive side, recent urban transport initiatives have resulted in successful new railways such as the Docklands Light Railway in London and several new lines that are part-railway part-tram. The delayed opening of the Channel Tunnel has provided a direct rail link between Britain and the Continent and has the potential to radically change the manner of long-distance goods transport.

The major growth in railways has, however, been that of nostalgia. Preserved railways have blossomed since the narrow gauge Talyllyn Railway in mid-Wales was rescued from closure in 1951 and reopened for tourists and enthusiasts. Since the 1960s and the end of main line steam, the number of such railways has increased tremendously, so much so that most of the dozens of rusting derelict steam locomotives awaiting scrapping at Barry, South Wales, have been rescued and restored. Now even diesel and electric locomotives are being restored as they too become redundant.

Part II: Civil engineering
3 Earthworks

The most underrated aspect of railway engineering has always been the earthworks — the cuttings and embankments — so necessary to obtain the steady gradients for the traffic on the line. The deepest cuttings and tallest embankments were all created by sheer hard work and muscle power, for it was only towards the end of the nineteenth century that steam power was harnessed for the job. The larger cuttings and embankments only represent a small part of the earthworks involved, for not a single yard of ordinary standard gauge track for steam powered railways could be laid directly onto the bare ground. Even on level surfaces the track had to be supported on a low embankment and arrangements made for its drainage — and in many cases it was flat areas, particularly those over mosses and unstable estuarine sands, that caused the engineers more trouble than the undulating uplands.

Simple earthworks were well established on medieval roads, usually consisting of no more than low embankments over muddy ground on the approach to bridges or shallow cuttings to ease the slope of a hill. On the early waggonways a more even gradient was required, but most of the early lines took coal down to navigable rivers — and later canals. Their steepness was not particularly important providing that it was reasonably easy to control the descending wagons by the primitive braking systems of the day — and not too difficult to haul the empty ones back up by man or horse power according to the gauge.

An easy continuous gradient all along such a line was not always easy to achieve, especially in areas where the valleys were steep-sided, such as the Shropshire coalfield. There is evidence in Shropshire that this was partly overcome by deliberately creating steep 'steps' between long stretches of relatively level track. At each step the wagon was simply lowered or raised to or from the next level. The process was probably adapted by the loading apparatus needed by the steep banks of the river at the end of the line

By the middle of the eighteenth century the self-acting inclined plane had evolved. These inclines between the levels had either a double track or a passing loop, but the principle used on each was the same. On these mineral lines most traffic was going downwards. A full wagon reaching the incline was attached by a rope to an empty one at the bottom, the rope being wound around a drum at the top. As the full wagon was lowered on one track, its weight helped to pull the empty one up on the other — a simple but ingenious solution to the problem. These inclined planes were sometimes, for

16   Railways of all kinds were usually given shallow embankments even on relatively flat surfaces to aid drainage and to protect their tracks. This was the case on this mid-eighteenth century waggonway serving the new, but short-lived, foundry at New Dale, Shropshire. The line can be seen curving towards the foundry, whose buildings later became a farm. Shortly after this photograph was taken in the summer of 1987, the whole site was bulldozed and the area open-cast.

obvious reasons, called 'winds' and by the end of the century, when used in conjunction with canals, not only reached epic proportions but also led to the first direct use of steam power to haul railway traffic — a generation before the successful introduction of the steam locomotive. They will be dealt with again later.

When a projected line was not simply built to carry goods downhill, then the engineering became necessarily more ambitious especially if hills and valleys had to be crossed. In *The Picture of Newcastle upon Tyne*, published in 1807, it was said that 'The first thing to be done in making a railway is to level the ground in such a manner as to take off all sudden ascents and descents, to effect which, it is sometimes necessary to cut through hills and to raise an embankment to carry the road through vales....'

The experience of these early railway builders also helped the canal pioneers of the eighteenth century, but they then took civil engineering literally to the new heights of excellence that made the Railway Age possible. Tolerances on canals were far less than those on railways, for obvious reasons. A canal has to hold water as level and as long as possible, so the 'cut' has to be made as flat as practically possible. This led initially to the meandering counter canals that studiously avoided too many cuttings or tunnels, but on most routes they were inevitable and engineering benefited as a result.

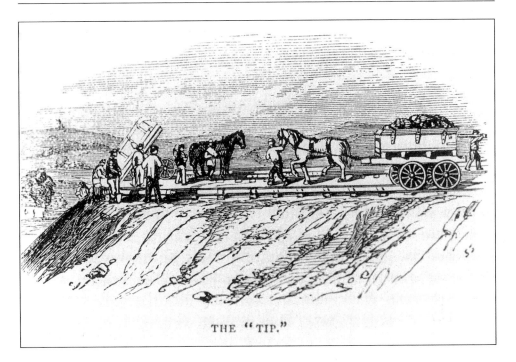

THE "TIP."

17   *The 'tip', a line drawing showing the simplest method of creating a cutting, taken from F. S.
      William's* Our Iron Roads *first published in 1852. The horse-drawn wagons full of spoil
      were simply run up to the end of the ever-lengthening embankment, turned, and unloaded.*

Already, by the start of the nineteenth century, many of the waggonways and tramways
were being built using techniques pioneered by the canals, so that when the first of the
steam railways were planned the manner of their construction was well established. All
that had changed was the scale of the enterprises, and of the engineering required. The
new lines were planned to follow more direct routes between A and B, and mechanical
engineering was still at a stage where the available locomotive power was quite weak.

The earliest steam powered lines had a ruling gradient — that is the steepest climb
allowed on the route — of around 1 in 300 but all efforts were made to have no gradients
at all. Locomotives were still in their infancy and even their main supporters — and
indeed pioneers — seemed to feel that their haulage capacities were relatively limited. The
ruling gradient on the Liverpool & Manchester was an amazing 1 in 849, apart from two
deliberately steep sections near Rainhill and rope-hauled inclines into the Liverpool
termini. On the much longer London & Birmingham Railway the ruling gradient was of
1 in 330, despite passing through the Chilterns. The route involved Robert Stephenson in
major undertakings such as the Tring cutting, nearly 2.5 miles long, and the Kilsby tunnel.
The gradient was still only made possible at the London end by originally stopping
locomotive haulage at Camden, and working the steeper section down into the Euston
terminus by rope-haulage and stationary steam engines. Only later was this section
locomotive hauled.

18   *Building railways through hilly terrain meant many cuttings and embankments, as well as steep gradients. The West Coast main line between London and Glasgow is largely without steep gradients or sharp curves until the Cumbrian hills. In the early 1980s BR put into service their revolutionary and unfairly ridiculed 'tilting trains', one of which is seen on a curving embankment at Crawford, Dumfries & Galloway, in 1985 (BR London Midland Region).*

By the 1840s improved locomotive design had allowed for slightly steeper ruling gradients which in turn helped to cut the cost of earthworks. Even so an engineer would occasionally overestimate the capability of locomotives and stubbornly insist on a steeper section to avoid a longer route; the best-known main line example in England is the Lickey Incline near Bromsgrove, Worcestershire. The 1 in 38 gradient was not really necessary but the engineer, Captain W. S. Moorsom, ignored the advice of far better engineers like Brunel and Robert Stephenson and did not consider even a minor deviation to avoid it.

Increasingly powerful locomotives did allow later lines to include steeper gradients but most of the main lines had been built by the 1860s. Trains on the last main line, the Great Central between Nottingham and London, easily dealt with a ruling gradient of 1 in 176. Nevertheless, it was not really until the full potential of electric power was realised that railway gradients ceased to be a problem to the civil engineers. The few new purpose-built high-speed lines in parts of Europe and Japan can have a ruling gradient unheard of in the last century without hindering the progress of new trains like the French TGV (Trains à Grande Vitesse) or the Spanish AVE (Alta Velocita Española). Despite the opening of the Channel Tunnel, such lines have yet to be built in Britain.

19   *Not a canal, but the trackbed of the former Cromford & High Peak Railway a little to the west of Middleton. The nature of the rock allowed the sides of the cutting to be left as undressed and unsloped stone. In the background is a short tunnel at a point where a cutting would have been a little too deep.*

Although tunnels and viaducts are the most spectacular parts of creating a reasonable level railway line, most of this is achieved by the simple earthworks. Wherever possible, routes were carefully surveyed to enable most of the spoil removed from the cuttings to be used in the formation of the embankments, a process known as 'cut and fill'. Long surveyed sections of the proposed line were usually produced for the engineer so that he could roughly calculate the volumes of soil involved. Where this was not possible, spoil from the cuttings had to be dumped elsewhere — often resulting in odd lumps and bumps on their upper sides. That was not as much a problem as a lack of material for the embankments, which usually meant either carting in spoil from long distances or digging out from areas adjacent to the track — resulting in otherwise unexplained 'cuttings'.

Common sense decreed that temporary tracks on the relatively level sections between the proposed cuttings and embankments were laid before any work on them began. Normally the cutting was dug not from the top but from the ends. A narrow trench was started on the line of the railway and gradually deepened and lengthened; this was known in some areas as the 'gullet'. When it was wide enough a temporary track would be laid in the base of the gullet and the spoil being dug was thrown into wagons to be taken away ready for the embankment. The sides were usually cut out in level steps before being evenly profiled. As the initial cut got deeper and deeper it would eventually be possible to

20   A L&NWR goods train in the early years of this century, hauled by one of the 4-6-0 '19in Goods' through a cutting with quite gentle slopes and more typical of most of those on main line railways. Note how pristine the recently-mown turfed sides were — a far cry from the present day.

lay one or more lines of temporary track on its floor and, on the longer cuttings, bring in steam locomotives to haul out larger wagons of spoil. This work was sometimes supplemented by man-powered barrow 'runs' up the sloping sides of the unfinished cutting and unloaded at the top to more wagons or simply in heaps. Working the 'runs' was a dangerous business.

The character of the cuttings depended on the soil and rock formations through which they were cut. The natural angle at which the material would not slip is called the 'angle of repose'. In good stone, the sides of the cuttings could be quite steep, almost vertical, without any form of masonry support walls. In soft and unreliable shales or clays, the sides had to be sloped quite shallowly to avoid the danger of slippage.

In some urban areas, especially in the centres of the larger towns and cities, the price of land encouraged railway companies to save money by minimising the amount of land needed for their cuttings by lining the narrowest possible track width with stone or brick revetment walls. In the difficult London clays the original cuttings into Euston station were revetted by walls seven bricks thick and they still caused problems until an inverted brick arch was built under the tracks to stabilise them. Other urban cuttings, such as those on the approaches to Birmingham or Sheffield, used up literally millions of bricks in their walls.

Sometimes walled cuttings would be needed in relatively small towns. When the North Midland Railway was routed though Belper, on the Derwent in Derbyshire, George

Stephenson had to build a stone-walled cutting though the middle of the town crossed by a disproportionate number of bridges to avoid cutting the streets. The result, opened to traffic in 1840, was, and is, rather grand.

On occasion the rock strata of a cutting could save the railway company a degree of expense. In several instances in areas of good quality building stone, a deep cutting was chosen instead of a cheaper tunnel because the additional costs were more than offset by the savings made on having otherwise to buy in stone for bridges and buildings from elsewhere. The fine sandstone from the deep Olive Mount cutting on the Liverpool & Manchester line was used for some of its bridges. Further south there was a tradition that the buildings in the GWR 'new town' of Swindon were built of stone from the Box tunnel. They are mostly of local Swindon limestone, but the softer stone used for window and door decoration does come from Box, probably from local quarries rather than from the tunnel. However, it would not have been impossible for the contractors to carefully quarry the cutting approaches to the tunnel instead of blasting it.

A more dramatic example is the Talerddig cutting on the former Newtown & Machynlleth Railway in mid-Wales, engineered by Benjamin and Robert Piercy. Nearly 40m deep it opened in 1863 when it was for a short while the deepest in the world. Its depth is emphasised by the fact that it was only built for a single line of track; the gradient is a steep 1 in 52 for over three miles leading up to and through it; a tunnel would probably have been cheaper to build but the company needed the stone the cutting could provide. During the construction of the Severn Valley Railway at the start of the 1860s a tunnel near Hartlebury was replaced by a 20m deep cutting to provide the necessary spoil for the embankments nearby; in this case a crude tunnel was dug from vertical shafts; the spoil was thrown down the shafts onto waiting trains of waggons in the tunnel — the exact reverse of normal tunnel construction but apparently an efficient way of constructing such a deep cutting.

All cuttings needed to cope with water. Springs could be cut during excavation and have to be tapped or gulleys built to cope with the outflow. After the cutting was finished, considerable but largely hidden drainage works in the form of drains down the slopes and alongside the track ballast, as well as culverts and soakaways, had to be built. They were usually lined with brick and had to be well maintained to avoid the risks of flooding. Incidentally, the accidental rediscovery of such drainage works is one of the unforeseen dangers on walking disused railway lines.

Some of the railway cuttings on the earlier main lines are major feats of engineering, particularly on the London & Birmingham Railway. The cutting between Tring and Castlethorpe is over 4000m long and averages more than 9m in depth; over a million cubic metres of material was removed by navvies using little more than picks and shovels. Most of this material was used to form the embankments to the north of it, six miles long, as well as several spoil dumps. The sides had to be quite shallowly sloped because of the nature of the local chalk so the effect of the engineering was rather diluted; the paraphernalia of the electric wires added in the 1960s have made it even less notable. The cutting at Roade, to the north, is a little more impressive even though it was later doubled in width; the original contractor gave up and steam engines had to be brought in to pump the many springs found during the excavations.

21   Bath is known for the elegance of the buildings made from its beautiful honey-coloured limestone, and no one can say that the Great Western Railway did not live up to the city's architectural standards in their route through the Sydney Gardens, part shelf, part cutting. A modern single diesel car approaches Bath in 1993 (Ken Hoverd/Archive).

One other type of cutting is the half-cutting or bench. Where a line follows closely the side or foot of a hill or cliff, a shelf is cut out of the hillside to provide a level surface for the tracks, often resulting in the removal of a thin sliver of the hillside above. Usually the upside of the bench has to be revetted in some way unless the rock is particularly solid. Typical examples of this type of earthwork can be seen on coastal lines, such as on the Chester & Holyhead line in North Wales and on lines in Devon and Cornwall.

One particularly dramatic example is at Dawlish, on the former South Devon Railway, where the cliff on one side is virtually perpendicular and over 60m high and the tracks are 10m above the beach. Another is at Vriog where, for over a mile, the Cambrian Coast line is carried on a terrace nearly 30m above the sea. Between Folkestone and Dover a whole cliff was removed to make way for such a benched section of track; the Round Down cliff, over 110m high, was blown up by William Cubitt, engineer of the South Eastern Railway, in the early 1840s — an act seen as the height of engineering excellence in its day but one that would now, thankfully, not be tolerated.

The use of shallow embankments to help roads keep clear of particularly marshy areas was already well established in the medieval period and would also have been used by the early waggonways. It would seldom have seemed worth building larger embankments on these lines until they began to tackle routes crossing over watersheds in the early eighteenth century. The earliest major railway embankment in the world is probably on the Tanfield line in County Durham, where the Beckley Burn embankment (or 'battery') is over 30m high and nearly 100m broad at its base; now covered in mature trees and undergrowth, it is difficult to appreciate its size. It was probably built a little before the famous Causey Arch nearby of 1727 and later took a standard gauge railway.

The engineering techniques involved in these early embankments were not particularly advanced or subtle. It was simply a matter of piling up the earth in a manner so that it would not slip. Indeed, few railway embankments from the eighteenth to the twentieth century were particularly complex structures. Long before the start of the steam railway boom in the 1830s, the artificial embankment in Britain had literally reached new heights in the late-eighteenth century canals. The sheer size of the southern approach embankment to Telford's soaring aqueduct across the Dee valley near Pontcystylte is usually overlooked.

As already mentioned, creating a railway embankment was usually combined with the excavation of a cutting, the spoil taken from the one being used in the other. Normally construction would begin at one or both ends of the proposed embankment, depending on the other workings of the route. In preparation, the turf and top soil along the area of the base of the embankment would be removed and stored for later reuse. Trees and shrubs on the site will be completely removed and usually the drains were laid on either side. The soil from the cuttings would then literally be tipped onto the ground and the earthwork gradually increased in height and length. The point at which the loaded wagons were unloaded was called the 'tip', for obvious reasons. Once the roughly profiled sides were complete up to the formation level, it would be covered with smoother top soils and, if possible, the original turves would be placed on the slopes to help consolidate them.

Drainage was important to avoid embankments being undermined. Culverts would be built at the base and along both sides. As most embankments were built across a sloping terrain, the function of the two side culverts was slightly different. Both took water from the land drains in the slopes of the embankment, but the one on the higher side also took the outflows of the field drains and surface water. This run-off would then be transferred to the culverts under the embankment and so through to the side drain on the other side and from there into the normal surface drainage of the area.

The sheer weight of embankments could lead to wholesale or localised sinking that had to be rectified before the permanent way was ready, and slippage of the slopes when first raised was also a common problem. Embankments across marshy areas proved particularly difficult and piling was used to support them. The most celebrated victory by a railway engineer over marshy ground is that of Stephenson's success crossing Chat Moss near Manchester. The embankment itself is only a few feet high and not at all impressive, but the achievement of building it was. Chat Moss was a peat bog just north of the River Irwell and the Liverpool & Manchester line crossed it for five miles of its route. Drainage failed to solve the problem of the moss and different techniques were needed. A heather 'road' was built to take a temporary narrow gauge railway that carried the materials for the embankment and its footings. Hurdles of brushwood, moss and earth, were laid on top of, and sank into, the bog until gradually an embankment finally appeared; ultimately

700,000 cubic yards of raw moss were used and the embankment was described as looking like 'a long ridge of tightly-pressed tobacco-leaf'.

Whilst the levels of the earthworks depended on the route chosen by the engineer, their width depended on the gauge chosen and the amount of lines required. Usually it was cheaper to build for a single line rather than a double, and for a narrow gauge rather than for a Standard or Broad one. Many lines were built to take two lines of track throughout, though only laid originally with one. The idea was simply that this would save initial outlay but, should the line prosper, then a second line could be added without the need to work on more earthworks and disrupt the first. The additional cost of building the earthworks for two lines was seen as well worth the investment.

For most of the lesser lines of the Railway Manias — and particularly on the second one in the 1860s — the second set of tracks remained little more than a possibility. Quite a few of the lines being built in the 1840s before the outcome of the 'Battle of the Gauges' was known, especially those supported by the Great Western (such as the Oxford, Worcester & Wolverhampton) were built to Broad gauge widths. Other companies, not sure which gauge would win, did likewise. These included the Shrewsbury & Birmingham Railway which, ironically, with the Shrewsbury & Chester, became the first Standard Gauge sections of the Great Western Railway soon after they were opened at the end of the 1840s — by which time the Broad Gauge cause had been lost.

4 Track

The railway track — rails, sleepers and all fixings — and the ballast which holds it in place is generally referred to as the 'permanent way'. As these are constantly being renewed it is a rather inappropriate term but it originated as a means of distinguishing it from the *temporary way* laid by the contractors during construction.

The earliest waggonway tracks were, like the planked runs used by the slightly earlier *hunds*, made of wood, a material that was extensively used in building and other engineering works. At the start of the seventeenth century, Huntingdon Beaumont's Nottinghamshire 'rayles' were certainly of wood, as were the 'fframes and Rayles' of Wilcox and Wells' 'artificial Engine' in Shropshire. The exact details of either are not known. Nevertheless both probably consisted of pairs of longitudinal baulks forming the road on which the waggons ran, held together by cross-members and bedded into the ground with an earth or stone ballast.

A slightly later description, of 1676, refers to the waggonways near Newcastle, which consisted of 'rails of timber...exactly straight and parallel'. By using rails such as this the waggons were not only given a smooth ride over the ground but their weight was spread evenly over each length of timber. The waggons had to be persuaded to stay on the tracks, of course. One of the earliest methods of achieving this seems to have been to cut a groove in the top of the rails in which the waggon wheels could run. Another simple method would have been to add timber guides, or flanges, on the outer or inner side of each rail to stop the wheels falling off; this seems to be shown in an illustration of 1588. In both cases the wheels of the waggons would have been of the same basic type as on road waggons.

It is not known when, or where, the guide flange was transferred from the rails to the waggon wheels. Several flanged wooden wheels were found in old workings of the east Shropshire coalfield during the nineteenth and early twentieth centuries, including one found near Broseley in the 1930s that was just nine inches in diameter. Certainly by the start of the eighteenth century it was more usual to have flanged wheels running on simple rectangular or square sectioned rails and that remained almost universal until the end of the century.

Standard track was made of good quality timbers, oak if possible, but beech or ash if not. There is an interesting 1764 description of waggonways near Tyneside by Gabriel Jars in the first volume of his *Voyages Metallurgiques*. He wrote that a typical route was:

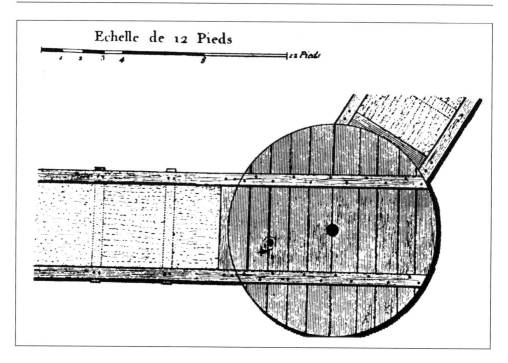

Echelle de 12 Pieds

12 Pieds

22 *Wooden waggonway track was both very simple but, by the mid-eighteenth century, quite
sophisticated. Gabriel Jars, a visiting Frenchman, provided a useful record of the lines of north-
eastern England, published in 1765. This drawing also shows one of the turntables. Note how
the rails — in this case single, rather than double — are pegged to the sleepers. The area
between the rails is built up to allow the horses a smooth running surface.*

'laid with pieces of oak....placed crossways at intervals of two or three feet apart
in which other well-squared and sawn pieces of wood, some six or seven inches
wide by four or five inches thick are fixed with wooden pins.....generally laid four
feet apart....'

A ballast of earth, stone or waste materials such as slag would then be added between the
rails up to just below the tops of the cross members (known as *sleepers* by the start of the
nineteenth century at least) to weigh the track down and keep it in place.

The distance between the two rails, the *gauge*, could vary enormously. Above ground it
tended to be between 4 and 5 feet in the north of England, about the same as the width of
a typical road waggon. In other areas, smaller gauges, of 2 to 3 feet, were often used. This
was the case in the east Shropshire coalfield before the Coalbrookdale Company began
their 'northern' gauge system in the 1740s.

A short section of mid-eighteenth-century waggonway track was salvaged from a coal
mine near Blanchland, County Durham, and is now preserved at the National Railway
Museum in York. The oak rails are 1.8m long and 900mm square, pinned to sleepers at a

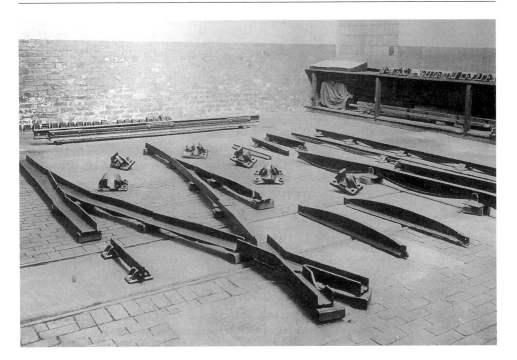

23   *The LNER began a small museum in the 1920s at York and in this display photograph some of their track collection has been laid out. In the foreground are plateway tracks and a switch or point; elsewhere there are sections of fish-bellied rail and straight rail of several kinds, along with track chairs etc.*

gauge of just 1ft 6in (a little under 0.5m); this was for the smaller underground waggons. In 1986 a small section of one of the Coalbrookdale Company's surface waggonways was excavated close to the Bedlam Furnaces by the River Severn and dated to the 1750s. The sleepers were fixed to the ground with wooden spikes and one had an unusual additional piece of timber laid on top of it which stopped a few inches from the heavily worn rails. The rails, laid to a gauge of 3ft 9in (1.15m), were dowelled to the sleepers by single pegs and the ballast was of furnace slag.

Wear and tear on the track, particularly after the introduction firstly of cast iron tyres, and then cast iron wheels in 1729, inevitably led to the need to replace broken or worn out rails from time to time and this required the removal of the ballast and often the sleepers as well. A simple system had evolved by the middle of the eighteenth century in which a second rail was laid on top of the first. This took most of the wear and could be replaced quickly without disturbing the rail beneath or the sleepers. Cheaper woods, such as sycamore or softwoods like fir, could be used for the bottom rails in the 'double rail' system as all they did was support the upper running rail.

An obvious development of the double rail was to replace the top wooden rail with one of iron. Iron strips had already been used on top of wooden rails in an effort to protect them, but the first complete iron rails, five feet (1.5m) long, appear to have been made by

24   *A section of relaid fish-bellied track of the former Cromford & High Peak Railway. Each rail is cast with the company's initials to help prevent theft and they are joined by cast-iron connecting chairs laid on top of the stone blocks. The blocks would have been mostly buried in the ground.*

the Coalbrookdale Company in 1767. So successful were these new rails that by 1774 the nearby Horsehay Works had produced 16,067 of them, slightly longer than the Coalbrookdale prototypes and enough for over nine miles of track. Iron rails were not cheap and a mile of line laid with them cost £800 even then; however, the savings in maintenance more than made up for the additional expense. It is claimed that the Caldon Canal line was the first railway authorised by Parliament that used iron rails, the Act being passed in 1776.

The next logical step was to dispense with the lower rail altogether and to spike the iron rail directly to the timber sleepers. Initially the iron rails seem to have been plain rectangular sectioned bars that were laid flat, but by the end of the eighteenth century it was far more common to lay them 'on edge'. Carpenters had known for two centuries or more that timber joists were stronger if they were taller than they were broad and the same was true of the new-fangled iron 'edge-rails'.

Iron was a far more versatile material than timber when it came to the production of rails. Cast iron could be made into virtually any desired shape or profile, as could wrought iron when it began to be used in the nineteenth century. Early experiments were made with different types of edge-rail, the most notable of which resulted in the 'fish-bellied' rail. Often attributed to William Jessop of the Butterley Company, and certainly used by him on the Loughborough & Nanpantan branch from the Charnwood Forest Canal opened in 1794, the design may be a little earlier. The rail was thin in section, except for a swollen top on which the wheels ran and a swollen foot over most of the profile; at the ends of the rail the lower section was wider and flatter where it sat on the sleepers. From the side, the central section of the rail was swollen to the 'fish-belly' shape to give additional strength to the rail between the supporting stone blocks or sleepers.

Several other different types of iron rails were being used at this time and experiments were made with different types of flanged wheels to run on them. In 1792 Thomas Dadford used cast-iron edge rails with slightly chamfered tops on a railway built by the Monmouthshire Canal; it is possible that these were designed for use by double-flanged wheels — similar to pulley wheels — and this was more obviously the case with the Measham line in Leicestershire of 1799 'wherein pulley wheels ran on metal ribs, cast on the bars'. Oval sectioned rails were also used, with single or double flanged wheels.

Another matter being addressed in the late eighteenth and early nineteenth centuries were the joints between the individual rails. Up until then simple butt joints had sufficed but if the two rails were not perfectly aligned there was a danger of derailment. With thick timber rails the risks were slight, but with thinner iron edge rails even small displacement could cause problems. In South Wales some edge rails were concave at one end and convex at the other so that where the individual rails met they could be slotted in to each other. In 1797 Thomas Barnes cleverly solved the problem of joining the rails and the problem of fixing the rails to the sleepers by using a small 'L-shaped' casting. The edge rails he used on the Lawson Colliery near Newcastle-on-Tyne were 'T-shaped' without a fish belly. Where rails joined, they fitted into a slot on the base of the casting, were butted together, and then bolted to its upstand. The bottom of the casting was pierced for a spike or dowel to fix it to the sleeper block. With this simple casting Lawson had developed both the *track chair* and the *fish-plate*.

George Stephenson and William Losh combined the best of these earlier ideas in their patent of 1816 for a fish-bellied rail fixed to stone sleepers in track chairs. The ends of the rails were joined by half-laps or curving scarf joints and bolted together in the chairs. This type of track was used on the Killingworth Colliery line.

The most important new design of rail in this period led to a completely new type of track, but one that, despite its initial popularity, proved to be something of a cul-de-sac in railway development. This rail transferred the controlling flange back from the wheel to the rail, resulting in an 'L-sectioned' casting. In these *plateways* or *plate railways* the wheels of the waggons had no flange and simply ran on the base of the rail. One of the supposed advantages of this was that ordinary carts could use the plateways and then leave them to continue on their way on ordinary roads. This seldom, if ever, happened and could only have done so if there was a common gauge — which was certainly not the case — and if there were many gaps in the flange to allow the trucks to travel between plateway and road.

Benjamin Outram, a partner at the Butterley Works with Jessop, is usually seen as the originator of this type of railway, also called, to distinguish them from the 'edge-rail' variety, *tramways*. The oft-quoted link between this name and Outram's is very dubious, especially as the words *tram* and *trammy* had been used centuries before in the coal industry, and 'tram' derives from the Germanic word *traam* — a length of timber. Outram was one of several visionaries who planned a national network of railways — or in his case, tramways. However, this type of track appears to have first developed not by him but by John Curr in the late 1780s. In 1788 plateway track was used on the surface for the first time for the inclined plane on the Ketley Canal in Shropshire, and for a line within an ironworks near Chesterfield.

In 1792 Outram was engineer of the Derby Canal and persuaded the company to use the plateway type of track on their proposed railway extension. The success of this led to a rapid expansion of the plateways, particularly in the English Midlands and South Wales. The form spread to Scotland as well, where at least one line — the Kilmarnock & Troon Railway of 1812 — used wooden versions of the rails; these were not a success and were replaced by cast-iron ones in 1815. Whilst plateways never became widespread after the introduction of steam locomotion, and many were either abandoned or converted, some survived for a remarkably long time. Outram's Little Eaton Tramway in Derbyshire, opened in 1795, continued to be a horse-drawn mineral line until it closed in 1908 and narrow gauge works plateways were still being used as late as the 1950s. The North East of England remained loyal to the edge-rail and was, in fact, rather slow to abandon its wooden waggonways as well.

It was probably on a plateway at Coalbrookdale that Trevithick's first railway locomotive ran in 1802, and the first successful trials of a second were held on another plateway at Penydaren in 1804. It quickly became apparent that the brittle cast-iron plates could not cope with the weight of the locomotive and many cracked under the strain. Cast-iron edge rails were stronger but still brittle and were not suited to the heavier weights that would be imposed on them with the coming of steam.

Wrought iron was expensive and even plating the timber rails added considerable costs to a line. Experiments with wrought iron rails would have been boosted by the development of Henry Cort's rolling mill of 1784, and wrought iron rails were made by a Mr Nixon in 1805 for a colliery near Newcastle-on-Tyne; unfortunately they were defective and had to be replaced by cast iron ones. The first commercially successful wrought iron rails were patented in 1820 by John Birkinshaw who had developed a special rolling mill to make them; these could be made as simple straight I-section rails or I-section with fish-bellies, and in lengths of up to 18 feet or more. Birkinshaw's patent even included the welding together of several sections of rail (though this does not appear to have been done), something not carried out on a large scale in Britain until the 1960s.

Compared to cast-iron rails they were still very expensive, but they were also strong enough to take the ever increasing weights of the new-fangled steam locomotives and the increasing size of the trains that these could haul. They were a vital factor in the development of steam railways and it was this type of rail that George Stephenson used for most of the Stockton & Darlington Railway of 1825 and the Liverpool & Manchester opened five years later.

Attempts to combine the assumed benefits of both the plateway and edge rail were made — in the form of *combination rails* that could take waggons with plain or flanged wheels. Such rails were used on the Ashby & Ticknall Tramway in Derbyshire and, as late as 1836, on the Rumney Railway in South Wales. They were expensive and impractical — and rare.

In general, as iron rails and plateways became more widespread, timber sleepers were being replaced by stone sleeper blocks that were considered to be longer lasting and

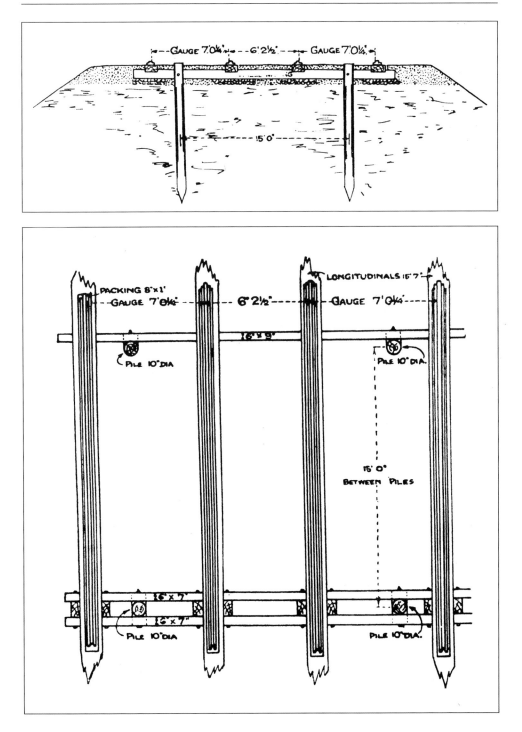

25　　*Plan and section of a typical double-tracked Broad Gauge main line, showing the system of longitudinal baulks to support the rails and the deep vertical piles holding them in place (from Track Topics of 1932).*

26   *With the demise of the Broad Gauge, the GWR sensibly found new use for redundant bridge rails. Sections were used as boundary markers and fence posts for post-and-wire fencing. This example is in west London but many more can still be seen throughout the former GWR system — which by the 1860s, had reached as far north as the Mersey (1999).*

steadier. Cast-iron sleepers were occasionally used, especially on lighter plateways, but were never widespread. The stone blocks were pierced by a fixing hole or holes in the top which usually took a tight-fitting wooden peg. A spike was hammered through the fixing hole in the rail, plate or chair into the wooden peg. The stone blocks were either laid square to the rails or in diamond fashion — the latter being seen as providing more continuous support for the rails. The size of blocks varied in size and weight, but were generally from 6–12ins (150-300mm) deep and could be up to 2ft (0.6m) square. For obvious reasons, these heavy stone blocks have survived in their thousands on long-forgotten railways when everything else has disappeared. There are particularly good runs of such blocks at Silkstone, Yorkshire, at Chapel Milton, Derbyshire, and Lydney harbour, Gloucestershire. In many areas the blocks can be seen reused in stone walls or buildings, their origins given away by the neatly drilled holes that took the fixing spikes.

Whilst the stone blocks were certainly longer-lasting than timber sleepers the additional support they gave to the rails was of no benefit at all. Timber sleepers 'gave' slightly but stone ones did not, increasing the strain on the rail and causing more breakages than would otherwise have been the case.

Despite this they continued to be used in the early years of main line steam railways. Stephenson had mainly used stone blocks on the Stockton & Darlington Railway in 1825 and, unusually, some other blocks made of elm. Although he then used transverse wooden sleepers on the Canterbury & Whitstable Railway opened five years later, this was probably because there was no good stone locally available for blocks. On the Liverpool & Manchester line of the same date he still used stone blocks for much of the route, but used timber sleepers on the section across Chat Moss. The sandstone blocks he used were prone to splitting and were soon replaced by more timber sleepers.

By 1837 it was becoming clear that transverse timber sleepers were far better than stone blocks and much of the London & Birmingham Railway was laid with them, even though stone blocks were still used for tunnels and cuttings on the grounds that they would be less susceptible to rot. These blocks were imported from elsewhere, being mainly Cornish granite or Whitby limestone. The problems of having too rigid a base for iron rails was demonstrated categorically on the Manchester & Leeds Railway (later the Lancashire & Yorkshire) after it opened in 1841; in a rock cutting the floor was dressed level and the iron rails were fixed directly to it. Within a few weeks it was clear that a normal ballasted track was needed. Few lines were built with stone blocks after then.

One well-known horse-drawn line dispensed with both timber and iron and used only stone rails. The 4ft 2in Haytor Granite Tramway in Devon, from the Haytor quarries to the Stover Canal, was opened in 1820. The rails were made of granite, cut to act as stone plateway track and even boasting quite complex pointwork. As late as 1835 a horse-drawn tramway was being built with granite 'rails' along the Commercial Road in London.

The important refinements in track design by Stephenson's former pupil, Joseph Locke, are often underestimated. The smooth running of his lines, such as the Grand Junction of 1837, was due to good quality engineering, the use of transverse wooden sleepers throughout, good ballast, and a different type of wrought-iron rail.

Even at the start of the 1840s a bewildering variety of rail profiles were still being used. By and large these were divided into four main types — the *single* and *double parallel*, the *flat bottomed*, and the *bridge*. The single parallel was like a skinny 'T' in profile whilst the double parallel was basically an I-sectioned rail, without fish-bellies with the head and foot sections of varying widths and symmetrical about the axis. The most important variant of this used by Locke was the 'double-headed' rail, developed with exactly matching top (*head*) and bottom (*foot*) bulges with a vertical section (*the web*) between. The intention was that once the top side had been worn the rail could be turned, thus doubling its life span. This never really worked, because the top would wear unevenly and the bottom would be already worn where it was in contact with the track chairs. A different form evolved with a different profile, one in which the head had been thickened out slightly and the foot reduced in size. The resultant rail became known as the 'bull-headed' rail and had become standard on the Great Northern Railway by the end of the 1860s. By the 1870s most major companies were using it, and it remained the official standard gauge rail on the British mainland until 1949. The weight per yard of rails varied but gradually increased throughout the nineteenth century to cope with the ever increasing loads they had to carry. In 1904 the main companies agreed an unofficial standard bull-headed main line rail that weighed 95lbs per linear yard.

Both double-headed and bull-headed rails were fixed to the sleepers in cast-iron track chairs. The basic design evolved slightly from the earliest forms and despite experiments

27   *The standard bullhead rail in chairs on wooden sleepers held in place by crushed stone ballast is still in use for most cross-country routes and has scarcely changed for over a century. This section of track and the points operated by a simple ground frame are at Aberystwyth, Dyfed.*

— such as Stephenson's complicated pin and ball arrangement on the Birmingham & Derby Railway in the mid-1830s — changed little. The track chairs were fixed to the sleepers in the early period by wooden pegs or spikes but both these methods were generally superseded by iron bolts by the later nineteenth century; the bolt-heads were below the sleepers and the nuts above for ease of tightening and removal. The slot in the chair for the rail was quite wide, allowing the rail to be wedged in place by wooden '*keys*', usually of a seasoned hardwood, generally oak although teak was being used in the early twentieth century. W. H. Barlow invented a wrought-iron 'key' in the 1840s but it was not used widely. Rails were not set exactly upright in the chairs, but leant in at a slight angle so that the flaring profile of the flanged wheels sat snugly on top of the head of the rail.

Until the late 1840s adjoining rails were secured in special double chairs but the development of the '*fish-plate*', short iron plates on either face of the web of the rails, spanning the joint and bolted through, eliminated the need for these. The plates could be adjusted to allow the small gap between the rails to be altered to cater for expansion in the sun or contraction in frost.

The massive demand for timber for sleepers threatened to exhaust domestic supplies of larch and Scotch pine and led to a huge import trade with North America and, in particular, with the Baltic from which millions of pine sleepers were imported. Techniques of treating these varied until the widespread use of creosote. The sleepers were generally laid on a stone ballast with additional ballast lain in between them — broken road stone or limestone being the most favoured. Other types of ballast were used

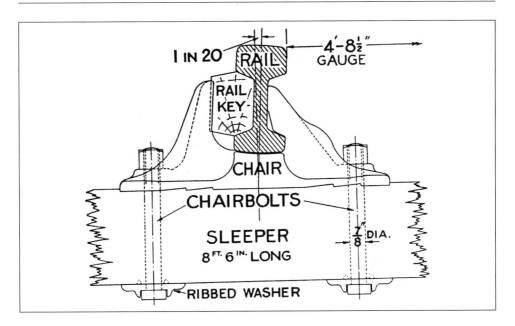

28   *A cross-section of the fixing of a bull-head rail in a track chair, published in* Track Topics *of 1932. The main difference today is that the wooden rail keys have been replaced by metal ones.*

by choice or necessity, including clay, small coal, and plain earth; an attempt to use concrete, on the London & Greenwich, was quickly abandoned and the line was reballasted in gravel by 1840.

This basic design of track — wrought-iron bull-headed rails laid in cast-iron chairs on timber transverse sleepers — would change little for a century and even now is used on many secondary lines. The main difference was the replacement of wrought-iron rails with mild steel ones following the introduction of the Bessemer converter, which revolutionised steel production. Successful experiments with steel rails were made by Robert Mushet for the Midland Railway at Derby in 1857 and by the London & North Western Railway at Crewe and London in 1862. The rails at Derby lasted until 1873 — far longer than any wrought iron rails. In 1866 the new Siemens-Martin Open Hearth method made steel production even cheaper and by the 1870s virtually all main railways were using mild steel rails that lasted far longer than wrought iron ones had done.

There was a brief attempt to revive the use of the wooden rail in the 1840s. William Prosser devised a system of using carriages with flangeless wheels running on rectangular timber rails; the carriages were kept on the rails round corners by pulley-like guide wheels angled to run on the top angles of the rails. The idea was to reduce the amount of friction and wear and tear on the track and to improve safety. After this system had, after serious consideration, been rejected for use on the Woking to Guildford line in 1844, Prosser continued to try to persuade other companies to use it on branch lines; he even set up an experimental line, complete with carriage, in 1845 on Wimbledon Common. Even William Cubitt was said to be in favour of wooden rails 'when the price of iron is high', but nothing

29   A South East & Chatham & Dover cast-iron track chair of 1901. The combined SER and
L&CDR companies later renamed themselves the South East & Chatham Railway, so this
chair was one of a relatively small batch; it ended its days in Shrewsbury! (1983).

much came of the experiment apart from a short and short-lived branch line in Paris.

Gauges in these early days of steam locomotion continued to vary. On the Stockton & Darlington and Liverpool & Manchester the Stephensons had used the local gauge of many of the railways in the North-east of England, which in turn was very much like the traditional 'gauge' of road-going carts and of the well-established waggonways. This was 4ft 8½in and would eventually become the national gauge for mainline Britain, most of Europe, North America, North Africa and parts of the Middle East, Japan, and Australia. Even so, in 1842 some of the main lines in Britain had different gauges and at the start of the 1840s there was a danger that there would be at least four different ones.

As well as the Standard (or English) gauge and Brunel's famous Broad gauge, several lines in the east of England were working to a 5ft gauge; these included the London & Blackwall and the Eastern Counties railways. In Scotland, a gauge of 4ft 6ins was popular and used on several main lines. Even the English Standard gauge had slightly different versions; the London & Brighton and the Manchester & Leeds railways both used a gauge of 4ft 9ins was, supposedly, meant to allow more leeway for standard gauge rolling stock — though the argument seems rather spurious. This could lead to rather odd situations. The Grand Junction was of true standard gauge, 4ft 8½ins; the Crewe & Chester was of 4ft 8¾ins; and the Manchester & Birmingham of 4ft 9ins. As all three lines met at Crewe this obviously led to potential difficulties in through working and the situation regarding gauges was not addressed properly until the Gauge Act of 1846 which insisted on the Standard gauge being used — apart from on the Great Western and its allies.

30   Since 1949 British Railways have seen the flat-bottomed rail as their main line standard. In the cold February of 1985 flat bottomed rails are unloaded at the Long Rail Welding Depot at Hookagate, near Shrewsbury, ready to be turned into continuous lengths up to 200m long. The depot, then an isolated outpost of the Western Region deep in London Midland Region territory, has since closed.

Brunel, of course, designed something completely different not only in gauge but in design from the standard track of the standard gauge lines. He could have used the same basic techniques for his wider 7ft (which 'grew' to 7ft and a quarter inch) Broad gauge; the only additional expense would have been in slightly heavier rail and slightly longer sleepers. Instead he designed a whole new form of track completely divorced from the standard gauge precedents. It was based on a different type of wrought-iron rail altogether.

The *bridge rail* has been variously described as a wide-brimmed hat or an upside down U in section. It was relatively lightweight and designed not to need track chairs; instead there were holes in the flanges and the rails were spiked directly onto longitudinal baulks of timber. Before those timbers were put in place, transverse timbers had been carefully put across the track bed after the ballast beneath them had been compacted. These transverse timbers were, in turn, fixed by beech piles driven deep into the natural ground beneath the ballast — which could mean that they were 30ft (9.1m) long on embankments. The ballast was used in the normal manner. After being laid in this way between London and Maidenhead, it was quickly found that the track settled between the

PICKING UP WATER AT FULL SPEED.

31   *This London & North Western Railway postcard of 1904 shows water troughs in use somewhere on the West Coast main line. The locomotive is one of Francis Webb's innovative but short-lived 2-2-2-0 three-cylinder compounds, probably one of the* Teutonic *class of the 1890s.*

piles, creating an uncomfortable 'roller-coaster' ride; things improved dramatically once the piles were cut away from the transverse timbers and the rest of the line was built without them. The transverse timbers were also dovetailed into the longitudinal ones.

The potential and actual chaos caused by having two different gauges in the main line railways of Britain led to the parliamentary Commission and the Gauge Act which in 1846 favoured the 'narrow' gauge. It did not, however, ban the Broad Gauge lines and the Great Western more than doubled their route mileage in the following decade. Other lines were laid with a combined Broad and Standard gauge track — the mixed gauge — over which both types of rolling stock could travel. This did lead to complications and expense at points, crossings and sidings and most were quickly converted to Standard Gauge. By the start of the 1860s few lines were being laid with the Broad Gauge, one of the last to be built being the Bristol & Portishead Pier & Railway branch in 1867; this was a short branch to a proposed new dock at Portishead. Elsewhere, other Broad Gauge lines were being converted to the Standard Gauge including the important South Wales Railway main line in 1872. Stubbornly, the Great Western Railway kept the Broad Gauge on their main London to Penzance line until 1892 when, in late May, over 200 miles of track were converted in a long weekend by over 4,000 platelayers.

After the Broad Gauge was finally abandoned the Great Western was left with a vast quantity of redundant bridge rail; much of this ended up being used as boundary posts and fence posts and thus travelled into many of the GWR areas that had never seen the 'seven foot' — on a system that by then extended to the banks of the Mersey and the Mid-Wales coast. Brunel seldom patented his inventions and did not patent the bridge rail. Other types of bridge rails were used on a few standard gauge lines on the same type of longitudinal timbers, examples including parts of the Glasgow, Paisley, Kilmarnock & Ayr line. A very similar rail was patented by William H. Barlow which had wider flanges. It was designed so that the rails could be fixed directly to the ballast without the need of the longitudinal baulks, and they were held 'at gauge' by wrought-iron cross-ties usually at 10ft intervals. It appears to have been used on Brunel's Broad Gauge South Wales line of 1844. When Barlow, then engineer of the South Eastern Railway, laid over 60 miles of his patent rails on its standard gauge main line to Dover in 1850 without permission, he was sacked.

Increasing standardisation of gauge and track at the end of the ninteenth century saw the almost universal adoption of the bull-headed rail, cast-iron chair, and timber sleeper. Whilst rails did eventually wear out, it was common practise to make the best use of them in two ways. One was to turn them so that the inner edge, which took the brunt of the wear from the flanged wheels, was placed on the outside. The other was to reuse worn rails off the main line on branch lines or sidings and marshalling yards. Cast iron track chairs proved to be particularly long-lasting. Even now on some sidings and little used branch lines, chairs over half a century old can still be seen. Chairs also tend to be moved around the system as they get older or lines are lifted. For example, on a recently closed siding in Shrewsbury once operated by the Shropshire & Montgomeryshire Railway, some of the track chairs, bought second-hand, bore the marks of the far away London, Chatham & Dover Railway and the South Eastern Railway and had mainly been made in the 1880s and 90s.

In the twentieth century experiments were made with iron and concrete sleepers and new forms of steel rail. The most significant change was the replacement of the bull-headed rail with the flat-bottomed type as the British Railways standard in 1949. Ironically, this revived a type of rail developed by Charles Vignolles at the end of the 1830s and widely used in most parts of the world apart from his native Britain. The new type of flatter chairs used for modern flat-bottomed rails can be fixed either directly to timber sleepers with 'elastic' steel spikes. Bull-headed rails were and occasionally still are used on minor lines, and are standard on the London Underground, but for most of these the old wooden chair keys were replaced by steel springs — modern equivalents of Barlow's wrought-iron ones.

In the 1950s pre-stressed concrete sleepers were also introduced in large numbers, first on the lesser used lines and then stronger ones on the main lines. When concrete sleepers are used, the chairs are held in place by steel clips known as 'Pandrols' after their inventor, Per Pande-Rolfsen — a Norwegian who patented them in 1957. Pandrols can also be used on wooden sleepers. Steel sleepers have not been as successful as yet. Apart from the advances made in track laying techniques, the most significant changes in recent years has been the widespread adoption of continuous welded rails. Such rails were tried in the 1930s but began to be used on a wide scale on main lines in the later 1960s. The future for track may lie in variants of PACT — Paved Concrete Track — which consist of continuous slabs of concrete that eliminate the need for both sleepers and ballast and thus reduce maintenance costs. So far they have only be used in small sections of urban lines and some short tunnels.

One related track feature in steam days was the shallow water troughs laid between the rails that allowed express locomotives to pick up water at speed. These were invented by John Ramsbottom, then Locomotive Superintendent of the Northern Division of the London & North Western Railway, in 1859 and tried in the following year at Mochdre on the main line from Chester to Holyhead. They were generally placed at 30-40 mile intervals and most main line companies adopted them. There were still 59 sites in use in 1956. Later, after the demise of steam power, some were retained on the East Coast main line to allow diesels to replenish their train heating boilers on non-stop runs.

5 Hybrid & rope-hauled railways

The huge success enjoyed by the modern railway was owed mainly to the development of the steam locomotive. Yet it is often difficult to remember that even when the Liverpool & Manchester Railway, the first of the truly modern lines, was approaching completion, steam locomotion was still only in its infancy and there were other two other equally important forms of power available. One was the reliable, but slow, horse, in use for centuries and hauling the passenger traffic on the Stockton & Darlington Railway; the other was rope haulage. Whereas there was no obvious way of speeding up horses or getting them to pull larger and larger loads, rope haulage could be, and was, improved by the steam power.

The first rope-hauled railways almost certainly developed quite early on in railway history. In *Le diverse et artificiose machine,* first published in Paris in 1588, A de Ramellis illustrates a double-tracked incline on which wagons are hauled by means of ropes turned by horse 'gins' at the top. In Britain this type of system was probably in use on the steeper inclines in east Shropshire and elsewhere by the later seventeenth century.

At first just manpower or horsepower in 'horse gins' would have been used. One of the largest to be constructed before the arrival of the canals was built for Ralph Allen of Prior Park, Bath. His main quarries were on Combe Down high above the wharf at Dolemeads on the river Avon. A wooden waggonway incline was built to connect a line from the quarries to the wharves and was opened in about 1731. The straight line of the former incline is now used by Ralph Allen Drive.

These early inclines also evolved into the self-acting inclines, as one waggon going down on one track helped to pull up another empty waggon on the other. On some inclines there was just one line of track and the two wagons passed each other at a loop halfway up. On others there were two tracks throughout. In either case the two were connected by a long rope which was wound around a drum at the head of the incline. These were, in effect, gravity powered rope-hauled railways, albeit on quite short steep sections.

With the expansion of the canal system in the late eighteenth century, the size of such inclines increased dramatically. In very hilly areas it was physically and economically impossible to build huge flights of locks over particularly difficult terrain. Such difficulties existed in the narrow gorge of the Severn at Ironbridge and Coalport. The main coalfield canals were built on the higher ground away from the valley, but the Severn was then one of the most important trading arteries in Europe. To get the goods carried by the canals to and from the river wharves required the construction of very large inclined planes indeed. Oddly, the first one of these in the coalfield was not connected to the river but with an

32   *The Middleton Incline on the Cromford & High Peak Railway was designed by Josiah Jessop and opened in 1831. The engine house, seen here in 1987, has been preserved and most of the trackbed is a footpath; the wagon stands on a short section of track that retains a length of wire rope over the sheaves.*

ironworks at Ketley and was designed by William Reynolds. The incline had two sets of plateway tracks, one of the first known surface uses of this type, and opened in 1788; it took tub-boats down the incline from the canal to the works in specially made cradles.

It was quickly superseded in scale by several others, Wrockwardine Wood, Windmill, and The Hay, on the Shropshire Canal, and Trench, on the Shrewsbury Canal. Opened between 1791 and 1797, on three of these the traffic was mostly downwards and they relied mostly on the self-acting principle. However, at the top of each there was a counter slope between the main incline and the top section of canal; the tub boats were floated into the wheeled cradles that were hauled, on plateway track, up the counter slope by a stationary steam engine. This engine could also supplement the gravity power on the main slope, and thus be considered to be the first use of steam power for a railway. Such a claim may seem rather tenuous, but the claim of the fourth plane for this accolade is much firmer. On the Wrockwardine Wood incline most of the traffic was upwards and thus almost entirely worked by the stationary steam engine at the top with little or no help from gravity. Opened in 1791 it was designed by Henry Williams and lifted tub-boats nearly 40m vertically from one stretch of the canal to another. The plateway tracks were later replaced by edge rails on all the inclines; Wrockwardine Wood was out of use by 1858 but that at Trench only closed in 1921. Standard gauge tracks have been relaid on the largest of them all, The Hay at Coalport; partially restored, it demonstrates the sheer scale of the engineering needed and the confidence of the age.

By the end of the eighteenth century several railways in hilly areas included quite sophisticated self-acting inclined planes along their routes and were being built in a similar manner to canals — with long reasonably level sections where possible and the occasional steep step, or incline, in between. Good examples of this stepped approach were Benjamin Outram's Peak Forest Tramway line near Chapel-en-le-Frith, opened in 1796, and the Froghall Railway engineered through the difficult terrain of the Staffordshire moorlands by John Rennie in 1802-3. Traces of both lines survive in the landscape. Traces of other inclines can be found in most of the hillier parts of the country. In the south-west, two inclines, at Murhill and Conkwell took Bath stone from local quarries to wharves on the Kennet & Avon Canal.

The precise date when steam power was introduced on an incline designed specifically to cope with railway waggons, rather than barge carrying cradles, is unclear but the earliest example appears to have been a 4ft 1in gauge tramway in Lancashire in 1803. In that year stationary steam engines were built to operate three inclined planes on the five mile long Preston & Walton Summit plateway built by the Lancaster Canal as a temporary means of connecting the two sections of their canal. Worked by a continuous chain these were probably designed by the tramway's engineer, William Cartwright. The most spectacular was that at Avenham near Preston, over 100m long with a 1 in 6 gradient down the steep side of the Ribble valley to a timber trestle bridge carrying the tramway across the river itself. The proposed canal link and aqueduct were never built so the 'temporary' tramway remained in use until the 1860s. Another early documented example of stationary steam power was at Birtley Fell incline near Gateshead, which was opened in 1809 to haul coal traffic.

By the 1820s steam-powered railway inclines had become generally accepted, though only on the more expensively engineered and more important routes. Most used simple Newcomen low-pressure steam engines, fairly expensive on coal but reliable and simple to maintain. As most were in coalfield areas anyway the fuel consumption was fairly irrelevant. A handful of the longer inclines had two steam engines, one at the top and one midway; one example was the short-lived Pont Walby incline on the Cefn Rhigos tramway, Glamorgan, opened in 1805 and closed by 1820. Most inclines had two tracks to allow waggons to be hauled up and lowered at the same time; others had just one.

The rope used on inclines would originally have been of hemp, but by the early nineteenth century iron chains were being used and these in turn were replaced later by wire rope. The changes in the type of rope at the Chapel-le-Frith inclined plane on the Peak Forest Tramway would have been typical; in 1809 a chain over 1000m long and costing £500 replaced hemp rope and was replaced in turn by wire rope in the 1870s. Usually the rope was run over a series of freewheeling iron rollers, or *sheaves*, sited at intervals between the rails.

The most spectacular and arguably the most successful of lines built using powered inclines was the Cromford & High Peak line, engineered by Josiah Jessop. Its act of 1825 authorised it 'to be propelled by Stationary or Locomotive steam engines or other sufficient power'. Opened in stages in 1831 and 1832 the level sections of the line were

33   *The slope on this railway underbridge is not an illusion; it takes the line of the former Nantmawr incline on the Shropshire/Powys border across the lane. This was the scene of Richard France's dangerous experiments with 'lithofracteur' in 1872.*

initially worked by horses until locomotives were introduced in 1833. The line crossed difficult terrain between Cromford and Whalley Bridge and included six inclines, the most impressive being that at Middleton Top, Derbyshire, with a gradient of 1 in $8\frac{1}{2}$ and nearly 700m long. This was still worked by steam when it closed in 1967 and the original engine and engine house has recently been restored. Three other inclines are worthy of note: the short incline at Whalley Bridge continued to be operated by a horse-gin until the line closed in 1952; the incline at Hopton was converted to locomotive haulage in 1877 and part of it, with a gradient of 1 in 14, became the steepest locomotive worked track in Britain; and the Sheep Pasture Top incline near Cromford became powered by an electric winding engine in 1964 a few years before it closed.

George Stephenson was an exponent of rope-haulage on several of the lines that he built in the North-east of England, having first built some inclined planes for the Killingworth Colliery in 1812. In 1819 he began work on the Hetton Colliery line, opened in 1822, which had five self-acting inclines — two worked by stationary steam engines; in between the coal wagons were worked by locomotives. By the time that line had opened Stephenson had been employed as engineer to the Stockton & Darlington Railway, which also included two inclines at Etherley and Brusselton on the line west of Shildon, and there were others on his Bowes Railway.

More famously, he also used stationary steam engines to operate inclines on each of his other early lines, the Canterbury & Whitstable and the Liverpool & Manchester, both opened in 1830. The three long inclines on the Canterbury & Whitstable were used by passenger traffic, and their three stationary steam engines meant that four of the six miles were cable hauled. The largest of the inclines was that up Tyler's Hill near Canterbury, over 3000m long on a gradient of 1 in 46. It was operated by two 25hp steam engines.

There were three inclines at the Liverpool end of the Liverpool & Manchester Railway. Two began operating when the line first opened and both were mostly in tunnels leading off the Chatsworth Road cutting. The shorter of the two led up to the original passenger terminus on Crown Street and the longer one, for goods only, descending through the much longer tunnel down to the Mersey wharves at Wapping. These were worked by a pair of steam engines housed in the once famous but long-demolished Moorish Arch; each engine house was 35ft long and 18ft wide and the engines had 24in cylinders with a six foot stroke. The incline to the docks was worked on a continuous rope but the rope used to haul the trains to Crown Street was returned by horse and cart! When the new station was built at Lime Street in 1836 it too was originally in a tunnel and worked by two new beam engines by Mather, Dixon & Co. housed in two new engine houses until locomotive haulage took over.

Despite the obvious benefits and capabilities of locomotive haulage demonstrated by the Stephensons by 1830, and especially by the success of their own locomotives, rope-haulage was still being recommended by both George and Robert Stephenson for some routes. Both men designed 'stepped' railways that made this necessary, rather than more direct ones that required more expensive engineering. George Stephenson engineered the Bolton & Leigh Railway, opened in 1828 and thus the first public railway in Lancashire, which had inclines at Chequer Bank and Daubhill powered by steam engines. Later, his Leicester & Swannington Railway of 1832 included inclines at Bagworth and Swannington and he was also involved in the planning of the first trans-Pennine route between Manchester and Sheffield which would have included several much larger steam powered inclines; that scheme was dropped in 1833.

Robert designed the Stanhope & Tyne railway on this principle, which opened in 1834; a later private branch off this opened in 1846 ended in an incline above the village of Rookhope and the standard gauge tracks by the Bolts Law engine house at the top were 1670ft (over 500m) above sea-level and claimed to be the highest in Britain. On the London & Birmingham main line, the last stretch from Camden to Euston station was also originally rope-hauled, even though it was only on a gradient of 1 in 77. The two 60hp low-pressure engines were supplied by Maudsley, Son & Field and had 43in diameter cylinders and a 4ft stroke. The endless rope, made by Huddart & Co. of Limehouse, was over 4000m long, weighed nearly 12 tons and cost nearly £500. The decorated chimneys serving the boiler houses were deemed by one contemporary to 'afford a fair sample of the approach to perfection which has in our times been made in this, as in many of other of the useful arts'. Their particular use was short-lived, as rope haulage was replaced by locomotive haulage in 1844.

Other engineers also built similar 'stepped' hybrid lines. Amongst these were two in eastern Scotland, both opened in 1831. The Edinburgh & Dalkeith had a 1 in 30 incline leading down to the Edinburgh terminus, 1100m long and powered by two low-pressure engines built by Carmichael of Dundee; it opened in July. In December the more ambitious Dundee & Newtyle Railway was opened across the Sidlaws with three inclines, one on the flank of the Law in Dundee, another near Auchterhouse, and a third just outside Newtyle near Hatton Hill. The steepest was the Law incline, 1 in 10 for over 1000m and worked by a high pressure 40hp steam engine; all trains were accompanied by a brake wagon in case the rope failed. Initially the inclines were the only steam operated sections of the line, the level sections in between being worked by horses until 1833.

From using rope haulage just on steep inclines it must have been a relatively short step to use it on more level stretches of track, though generally horses were deemed to be cheaper and as efficient. One of the best examples of a relatively flat rope-hauled line was the Brunton & Shields railway opened in 1826, which used a cable system devised by Benjamin Thompson. When the Liverpool & Manchester line was being built, there were still serious proposals to make it cable-hauled in the same way, even backed by such engineers as James Raistrick; the success of the Rainhill trials of 1829 persuaded the directors that locomotive power could be used throughout — apart from the inclines in Liverpool.

Nevertheless George Stephenson later recommended that the four mile long London & Blackwall Railway, built mainly on viaducts, should be cable-hauled — one of the reasons being that it would avoid any problems of cinders from the locomotives causing damage to people or property in the densely populated area through which the line ran. Engine houses were built towards each end of the line, at the Minories and in Blackwall, to house marine condensing steam engines. There were no trains of carriages as such. Instead, individual carriages were assigned to individual stations on the route and attached to the continuous rope. At a given time the engine at the Minories would be put in gear and each carriage then moved independently westwards until meeting up temporarily at the terminus. For the return trip, the Blackwall engine would operate and the carriages would start off as a loose train but each carriage would stop at its own station until there was only the Blackwall carriage left. This system started in 1840 and was extended to Fenchurch Street in the following year; locomotive haulage replaced it in 1849 and the original 5ft gauge tracks were converted to the Standard gauge at the same time.

Although the occasional steam powered incline was still built after this date, they were usually for very specific purposes and not built to be parts of a longer railway. The last rope-hauled passenger traffic was that at Cowlairs in Glasgow which ceased in 1908. Other inclines, both self-acting and steam powered, continued to be built for industrial purposes — often associated with quarries — and there were several oddities scattered about the country.

One of the larger self-acting mineral inclines was that built by Richard Samuel France in 1866 on the Shropshire/Powys border to link his quarries in the hills at Nantmawr with a branch line of the ill-starred Potteries, Shrewsbury & North Wales Railway. It was over 500m long with a gradient of 1 in 8 and carried two lines of track; it crossed a minor road on a girder bridge as well. Descending wagons were controlled by a brakeman at the top. In 1872 it was the scene of a remarkable demonstration. France had been experimenting with a German explosive called lithofracteur in his quarries and had attracted the attention of the War Office. To show how safe it was, he tied some to the buffer of a mineral wagon at the foot of the incline and allowed another to be released from the top, unbraked. In the resulting collision, there was no explosion — but France had been lucky. In later secret tests at the Woolwich Arsenal it was found that lithofracteur was unstable, and potential more lethal to its handlers than to the enemy.

At the end of the nineteenth century there was a vogue for building other rope-hauled railways, mainly for pleasure. These included a wide variety of funiculars and cliff railways, often at least partially self-acting and some powered by the hydraulic balance system. This simply used water tanks below the carriages that were filled to provide weight for downward trips and emptied for the upward ones. A much earlier example had been the incline at Beck Hole on George Stephenson's Whitby & Pickering Railway, opened in 1835 for horse-drawn traffic; the original water counter-balance system was not too successful and was replaced by a stationary steam engine long before the incline was bypassed in 1865. Typical late nineteenth century funiculars include the former Clifton Rocks Railway near Bristol, opened in 1893 and closed in 1934; the Bridgnorth Cliff Railway, Shropshire, opened in 1892 and still in operation though now converted to electric working; and a much more recent one built at the Centre for Alternative Technology at Machynlleth.

Tracing the remains of inclined planes is generally not difficult. Hiding several hundred yards of carefully constructed even gradient in the landscape is not easy without major earthmoving and even the most overgrown example can generally be identified. Remains of the track, the rope 'sheaves', and their bearers are generally scarce, although some of the earlier inclines have retained their stone sleeper blocks. Often these are buried beneath the grass or can be seen reused in adjacent drystone walls or stone buildings. The degree of survival of the engine houses, boiler houses, chimneys and drum supports at the head of an incline depends entirely on what happened to the line after it was either abandoned or converted to locomotive haulage.

6 Atmospheric railways

An alternate means of using stationary steam engines for railway propulsion was taken very seriously in the 1840s. Instead of using ropes attached to the trains, this system involved harnessing the power of the vacuum to create, according to the more romantic of its supporters, a 'rope of air'. The atmospheric railway was not, as is often thought, another creation of Isambard Kingdom Brunel, despite usually being associated with him.

As early as 1812 George Medhurst had published a pamphlet outlining his idea of placing a carriage within a tight-fitting tube and exhausting the air in front of it by a steam powered pump to create a vacuum. The normal atmospheric pressure acting on the rear of the carriage should then in theory, propel it along. Medhurst then considered it more practical to build a much smaller tube with a piston inside it that was attached to the carriage above, a scheme he revised in 1827 claiming that speeds of up to 60mph were possible. Clearly the wheels of such a carriage would have to run on rails of a sort and thus would qualify this as a railway. However, there is no evidence that anything came of it.

The basic concept was taken up a few others, including J. Vallence who planned a short line in Kensington, but it was seriously developed for the first time by three men, Samuel Clegg and brothers Jacob and Joseph Samuda, who patented their much improved version in 1838. A continuous iron tube was laid in the middle of normal railway track and contained the tight-fitting piston. Pumping engines were built at intervals of about three miles along the route and the steam from them created a partial vacuum in front of the piston, causing it to move. The piston was attached by a connecting rod to a small truck or van, which in turn was connected to the carriages. As the piston moved so did the train.

The potential benefits of the system were manifold. The fact that no locomotives were needed meant that the civil engineering on the routes did not have to cope with traditional weights, gradients or curves and much cheaper routes were possible; railways could be built through fairly rugged terrain without too much expense; the running costs of the stationary steam engines would be much cheaper than those of expensive and mechanically complex locomotives that had to propel their own weight as well as that of their trains; and passengers could be assured of a faster and smoother ride.

Unfortunately, before any of that was possible, the connection between the piston and the carriage obviously had to pass through the tube and making the necessary continuous slit in the top as airtight as possible proved to be the system's Achilles' heel. Leather, reinforced by strips of iron, was the only viable method of closing this 'longitudinal valve' at the time. And it didn't work. The leather got wet or dried out or was even gnawed at by rats.

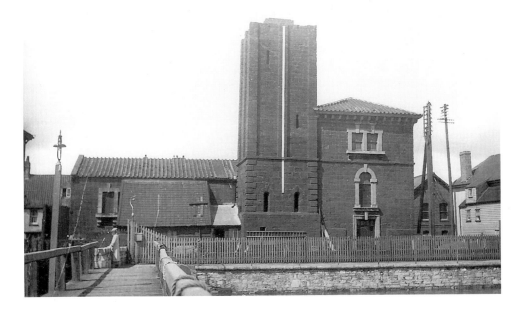

34   Relics of the ill-fated atmospheric railways are now few. This is the Starcross Pumping station in Devon, one of several built by Brunel to provide the necessary vacuum in the pipes that powered the trains. Built, to a typical Italianate design, in 1846 it quickly became redundant and the tower has lost its 'campanile'. It now houses a small museum.

Brunel had considered using the atmospheric principal through the fairly steeply graded Box tunnel as early as 1840 and was involved in some private experiments with the Samuda brothers on a mile or so of track on what became the West London Railway at Wormwood Scrubs; the public were allowed to ride on some of the trains. In 1841 it was suggested by James Pim that it should be used on a small branch line in Ireland about to be built from Dalkey to Dun Laoghaire (then briefly called Kingstown), engineered by Charles Vignolles. This was finally agreed in 1843 and the line was officially opened to traffic in 1844. Inevitably it was monitored closely by many engineers — who often reached totally different conclusions. Robert Stephenson, who had been asked to consider using it on the Chester & Holyhead line, thought it unworkable; Isambard Kingdom Brunel, on the other hand, was enthusiastic. He managed to persuade the board of the new South Devon Railway to adopt it on their 50-odd mile route south of Exeter that he was just about to build.

Before that line was ready for traffic, the atmospheric railway had entered revenue earning service in Britain on the London & Croydon Railway's extension to Epsom, Surrey, engineered by William Cubitt. Passengers were allowed to ride on trains unofficially in the late summer of 1845 and officially in the following January. Cubitt designed vaguely Tudor Gothic engine houses along the route for the pumps which exhausted a tube 15 inches in diameter. However, the system on this line was soon doomed — not just because of any inherent problems within it but because the company became part of the London, Brighton & South Coast Railway who had no interest in developing an unproven and as yet unreliable system.

On the South Devon Railway the engine houses were designed by Brunel himself and built in an Italianate style. Difficulties abounded; the original 13in diameter tubes ordered by Brunel were replaced by 15in ones and the planned engines could not cope and needed to be upgraded. When the line opened in stages to Newton Abbot in 1846 the company had to hire locomotives to work it. It was not until the September of the following year that revenue earning atmospheric powered passenger trains were running between Exeter and Teignmouth and they did not reach Newton Abbot until January 1848.

Further expansion of the system was put on hold, even though some of the engine houses had been built and the tubes delivered. When all went well the trains could travel at nearly 70 miles an hour but the problems of maintaining the leather valve, plus other technical difficulties, proved too much and Brunel admitted defeat in the summer. The line reverted to locomotive working throughout in September 1848. The venture severely but temporarily damaged Brunel's reputation and cost the railway's shareholders nearly half a million pounds. It also left a legacy of steeply graded track on a Great Western Railway main line, the steepest section, at Dainton, being on a gradient of 1 in 36.

Two of the South Devon engine houses, at Starcross and at Totnes (which was never actually used) survive. On the Croydon line only the section between West Croydon and Forest Hill was commercially worked on the atmospheric principle and this stopped in 1846; the Dalkey branch reverted to locomotive power in 1854. None of the other schemes of the Railway Mania that tried to climb aboard the atmospheric bandwagon — from the sensible Direct London & Portsmouth line to the bizarre London & Holyhead & Porth Dynlleyn Railway that planned to spend £2,500,000 building a line from the capital and through Snowdonia using 'Pilbrow's Atmospheric Principle' — were ever built. James Pilbrow's system, published in 1844, used the action of the piston in the vacuum tube to turn geared capstans placed at intervals between the rails that connected with a geared rack under the carriages and thus propelled them along.

The last serious attempt using the Atmospheric principle was at the Crystal Palace, Sydenham, in 1864, where a working model of T W Rammell's 'Pneumatic Railway' was demonstrated to the public on a 600-yard length of Broad gauge track partly within a brick-built tunnel. Reviving Medhurst's original idea, the carriage itself formed the 'piston' and the tunnel the tube. As well as the air in front of the carriage being pumped out to create the vacuum in one direction, air was pumped in to propel it on the return. It was successful enough to lead to the formation of a company to build an underground line from Whitehall to near Waterloo station. The section from Whitehall was in a brick-lined tunnel to the side of the Thames, and from there it would run through an iron tube beneath the river to Waterloo. This would have been the first proper 'tube' in London. Although the tunnel section was started in 1865 and almost finished, the scheme was abandoned in the financial crisis of 1866; the unfinished tunnel is still in existence.

7 Bridges

In Britain railways were usually built across well-established and well-peopled landscapes. They had to cross both natural barriers, such as rivers and streams, and man-made features, such as roads and canals. In addition, the railways had to provide access over or under their new lines to retain the historic links between parts of large estates or farms. All this required the construction of tens of thousands of bridges, ranging from ones that were little more than glorified culverts to civil engineering masterpieces such as the Forth Bridge. As a very rough estimate, there were at least $2\frac{1}{2}$ bridges for every mile of track, and bridges are the most common of all railway-related structures.

In general there are just two main categories of bridges — those that carry the railway over something and those that carry something over the railway. The former are known as *underbridges* and the latter as *overbridges*. To slightly confuse matters, on those relatively few occasions where one railway crosses over another, one line's underbridge is the other line's overbridge — but these are usually called *intersection* or *flyover* bridges.

The difference between a *bridge* and a *viaduct* is not always easy to determine. Technically, the word *viaduct* is an Anglicised version of the Latin words *via ducta* 'a way conducted across' and it was probably coined as a direct parallel to *aqueduct*. It only came into common usage in the early nineteenth century. Usually, the word is deemed to mean a multi-arched bridge carrying a road or railway across a valley or river, distinguished from a mere bridge by the number of its arches. Technically this would mean that some of our more famous railway *bridges* — such as the Tay Bridge, the Barmouth Bridge and the Royal Border Bridge at Berwick — are really *viaducts*. The difference between the terms is not really important, but one simple distinction could be that a bridge is designed to cross some specific localised feature, like a river, road or railway, whereas a viaduct carries a railway across larger geographical features, such as a broad valley or through a town.

Most of the earliest waggonways and plateways were built at a time when there was not a great deal of road traffic and, being small local enterprises were built relatively cheaply, wherever possible roads and paths were crossed on the level — at level crossings. Natural obstacles, such as streams and valleys, still had to be crossed and most of the surviving railway bridges of the eighteenth century were built for that purpose. Things had changed little by the arrival of the earlier steam railways but as both rail and road got busier, level crossings became less and less desirable — though often unavoidable.

Although cheaper to build, level crossings over public roads had to be manned — and were potentially dangerous. This fact soon led to governmental pressure being exerted to

35   *At first sight this looks to be a simple road bridge — but over another road. In fact it was built in 1802 to carry the Ticknall Tramroad over a road just outside the Derbyshire village of that name. It is built of local rubblestone with brick voussoirs in the arch.*

use over or underbridges wherever a railway and public road crossed. Generally, unless the railway was already on an embankment, it was cheaper to build an overbridge.

The simplest way to build an overbridge was to place it at right-angles across the railway, thus using the least amount of materials. To save money if the road and railway did not cross at right-angles, the railway company would often build its bridge at right angles anyway and have embanked approaches on either side carrying the traffic up to it, coping with the resulting 'S-bend' before descending down the other ramp. Where road and railway were almost parallel before they crossed, both turns at bridge level would be virtually at right angles. Similar layouts were used for roads passing under the railway. When traffic was light and travelling no faster than the walking pace of a horse, these diversions seldom mattered. Today, in an era of high-speed motor traffic, many of these bridges have become accident black spots.

Not all bridges could be built on the cheap like this. Where a railway crossed over a canal, for example, it was difficult to alter the line of either and if the crossing was not at right angles the bridge would have to be built on the 'skew'. This was also the case where a railway crossed a well-established main road, or a river. If the bridge was a girder bridge the problem to the contractors was slight; however, if a brick or stone arch bridge was needed, then the skills of the bricklayers or masons were tested and the manner of the construction of the arch carefully worked out in advance.

Railways had a duty in law to preserve rights of way whether they were roads or footpaths. Level crossings became frowned upon by the Board of Trade for roads unless the construction of a bridge was impracticable. Pedestrians of relatively little used footpaths had to make do with wicket-gated level crossings and it was only on very busy paths, usually in towns, that footbridges were provided, usually of the same type as those used at stations. At Rainhill, on the Liverpool & Manchester Railway, there are two footbridges — one for the use of passengers and the other, at the east end and fenced off from the platforms, taking a public footpath across the tracks; both were probably built in the later nineteenth century.

As well as the normal *public* bridges over or under public roads and lanes, there were also those built for private access, especially where a railway cut through the lane to a farm or a drive to a house. These are termed *occupation bridges* as they were retaining the owner's right of occupation of his established lane or track. Another type of non-public bridge is the *accommodation* or *field bridge* designed to allow the free interchange of farm traffic and livestock between parts of an existing farm separated by the railway. These were not necessarily built on the line of existing lanes, but built at convenient points once the route had been established. As with occupation bridges, these tend to be narrower than public bridges, designed only for limited traffic. The most basic of these is little more than a low-roofed subway under the tracks, known as a *cattle creep*.

Occasionally, railway builders were presented with an unusual bridging problem that had to be overcome. Some of these were associated with existing canals. Normally, railways crossed over canals but in some instances had to go under them. This meant the need for an aqueduct as an overbridge, and usually, for a temporary aqueduct to be built first to allow canal traffic to continue whilst the permanent one was being constructed. Alternately, the line of the canal could be diverted towards the new aqueduct instead. Near Carreghofa, Powys, the abortive main line of the Potteries, Shrewsbury & North Wales Railway passed under an arm of the Shropshire Union canal and a road. A temporary timber aqueduct was built just north of the canal line and the canal was diverted to this until the main aqueduct was ready in 1868. The timber structure was then removed, but the earthworks of the approaches to it can still be seen. The aqueduct consists of a trough of wrought-iron on bolted wrought-iron girders supported by cast-iron pillars; the adjacent road bridge is a simple brick arch. At Brownhills, West Midlands, a more elegant cast-iron aqueduct of 1850 carries the Anglesey Arm of the Birmingham Canal Navigation over the South Staffordshire Railway; here, railway and canal were built at the same time and by the same engineer, John Robinson McLean.

Sometimes a railway viaduct would be at a high enough level to easily oversail existing road bridges beneath it. On rarer occasions the difference in levels may be much less and the decision was made, on practical and economic grounds, to rebuild the older bridge to accommodate the new. Practical and economic grounds were not always good enough. For example, when building a bridge to take the Inverness & Perth Junction Railway over the River Garry at Calvine, the company was unable to persuade the local landowner, the Duke of Atholl, that the old road bridge over the river should be replaced and the road diverted. Instead, the engineer, Joseph Mitchell, was forced to build a bridge of three arches, two 40ft (12m) wide flanking a central arch of 80ft (24m), that crossed both the river and the old bridge at an angle. On the Brentford branch of the Great Western Railway there was an even more convoluted arrangement in Southall, where the line crossed under a canal *and* a road bridge; in this case the railway company had to build all three bridges.

36   *The Lee Dingle bridge carried a plateway over a deep valley, and the London & North Western's branch railway to Coalport of 1861. It is a tall lattice girder structure and surprisingly elaborate — and expensive — for a simple plateway. This view was taken in 1983.*

The design and materials used for a bridge were not just dictated by economy or by the company's house style. In many cases landowners managed to persuade the railway company to embellish a bridge on the route as part of the agreement for selling the land to them in the first place — the additional costs to the company being relatively minute compared to complicated changes in route or litigation.

Materials

Up until the mid-nineteenth century most railway bridges were built of fairly traditional materials — timber, stone and brick — but quite early on in the steam age the possibilities of 'new' materials such as iron — wrought or cast — had been realised. Later, steel replaced iron, and by the start of the twentieth century concrete was also being used for quite major structures. Different types of materials could be used in the same bridge, and typical *composite* structures included the use of stone and timber or iron and brick.

37   *The simplest bridge of all — but still a necessary one; the timber baulks carry the tracks of the Nantmawr quarry line over a small brook on the Shropshire/Powys border. The main baulks carry planks on which the ballast was laid. The line had been closed for many years by the time of this 1987 photograph, but the rails are, unusually, still* in situ.

Timber

The very earliest bridges carrying waggonways across rivers or ditches were almost certainly made of wood, though none of these are known to survive. Timber remained an important building material for bridges — and for much else besides — well into the era of the steam railway, though it enjoyed far greater popularity and, literally, reached far greater heights in other parts of the world — particularly in North America.

Bridges constructed entirely of timber tended, in Britain, to be relatively small in scale, often used simply for accommodation bridges and footbridges. If the span was narrow enough, the 'bridge' could consist of little more than long horizontal beams laid between masonry abutments. As most spans for railway bridges are usually too wide for this, the majority of timber bridges had to be built of a large number of separate timbers jointed together. The use of trusses in the roofs of wide buildings had been developed for centuries and the trussed timber bridge developed directly from them.

Despite their use by engineers such as Brunel, in Britain most timber bridges were generally seen only as temporary expedients to be replaced as soon as possible by more durable materials. Building in timber did allow bridges to be built far more quickly at far less cost but they were seldom seen to be permanent structures. Nevertheless, several did last for many more years or even decades than expected — two timber viaducts built by Brunel near Aberdare on the Vale of Neath Railway's Broad Gauge colliery line, opened in 1854, were still in use in 1939 and not pulled down until 1947. Parts of the substructure of Brunel's much rebuilt bridge on the South Wales Railway at Loughour, built in 1852, may be original.

Quite often companies would build the abutments for the less important overbridges, and particularly for accommodation bridges, in masonry but the arch in timber — rebuilding that part in brick or stone as funds permitted. The evidence for this can often be seen in surviving bridges, where the abutments are of stone and the arches of brick — though it was not unknown for such composite construction to have been used from the start. If the type of bricks used are obviously later than the date of the opening of the line then there is a strong possibility that the original arch has been rebuilt. This was not just confined to smaller bridges. On Henry Robertson's great stone viaduct carrying the Shrewsbury & Chester's 1848 main line across the Cerriog at Chirk on the Shropshire/Clwyd boundary, alongside Telford's earlier canal aqueduct, the approach arches were originally of laminated timber before being replaced in stone. As he anticipated this change and designed the bridge accordingly, the traces of the earlier arches in the surviving fabric are virtually impossible to see — apart from slight differences in the parapet and a lack of keystones in the newer arches.

Cases in which a masonry bridge was superseded by a timber one are very unusual — but several were recorded. One involved a rare miscalculation by no less an engineer than Brunel. The success of the shallow brick arches of his Maidenhead bridge on the Great Western main line had confounded his critics, but the even flatter arch of a bridge over the River Parrett on the Broad Gauge Bristol & Exeter Railway, completed in 1841, began to collapse when the timber centring was removed. As a result the masonry arch was dismantled and replaced by laminated timber ribs which survived until 1904.

At the other end of England a two-arched masonry bridge over the River Tyne at Linton on the newly opened North British Railway was swept away in a flood in 1846. The stone abutments survived virtually unharmed and, desperate to get the line reopened as quickly as possible, the company erected a very simple, but very effective, single span timber bridge between them. In 1861 a landslide severely damaged the new viaduct at Buxworth, Derbyshire, on the Midland Railway's cross-Pennine line just before passenger services were due to start. A temporary trestle timber viaduct was built on a slightly different alignment next to it and survived for several years before being rebuilt.

Despite being one of the most visionary of engineers, Brunel was one of the few in his time that continued to see timber as a useful material for railways. This was possibly due to his innate distrust of cast iron for bridge building and also his need to cut down on costs on many of the projects in which he was involved. Nevertheless, it is worth remembering that he originally considered crossing the Tamar between Devon and Cornwall with a timber bridge — a feat that in some ways would have been even more remarkable than the bridge he eventually did build.

Brunel's first exercise in timber bridge building was probably the overbridge crossing the Sonning Cutting on the GWR main line near Reading, built in 1841 but later replaced. This had five timber spans carried on four timber trestles and was the prototype for many

38   Brunel's timber bridges looked decidedly spindly and lightweight, but many survived in use for half a century or more. This example was at Truro, Cornwall, on the Cornwall Railway, opened in 1859. Over 400m long and 30m high it was replaced by a new masonry viaduct in 1904.

of his later timber bridges. However, his first major timber bridge proved to be unlike any of those that are generally associated with him. The GWR main line through much of Bath runs on a long multi-arched masonry viaduct, and crosses the Avon on a skew bridge. In his original designs, this bridge was to be a two-arched wrought iron structure, and the materials had even be ordered when, with time as usual pressing and no suitable contractor available, Brunel decided to build in timber instead. Each of the two 24.4m arched spans consisted of six timbers laterally trussed and tied ribs made up of laminated deal planks bolted and strapped together. The outer spandrels were infilled with decorative cast-iron. Opened in 1840, this remarkable bridge survived until 1878, when it was replaced by a much more mundane iron girder bridge that was itself replaced in 1959.

The more typical 'Brunel' bridges were the fragile looking viaducts of his Broad Gauge ventures mainly in Devon and Cornwall, although others were also built in Gloucestershire and South Wales. Brunel experimented with the structural capabilities of timber and also with standardisation of the various parts to facilitate maintenance and replacement. He ensured that all timber used was 'kyanised' — treated with a solution of bichlorate of mercury invented by J.H.Kyan to arrest decay. There were no less than nine timber viaducts on the Great Western Railway's Swindon to Gloucester line between Stroud and Frampton, one, at Slip, having 22 spans of 30ft (9.1m) and another, at Capel's, 18 such spans. Finished by 1845, these varied in design according to their size and location but all used sophisticated trussing of relatively short timbers strengthened in some cases by iron tie-rods and support plates. They were replaced from 1859 onwards.

The South Devon Railway bridges were the most dramatic, spanning the deep valleys of small tidal rivers heading for the sea. They were composite structures, with soaring and tapering narrow stone piers rising to track level and carrying the trussed timber arches. The most dramatic was at Ivybridge, built on a curve and with a highest part 30m above the ground. Brunel's loading calculations seem to have been for the weights of his abortive atmospheric system abandoned before the line was open. To cope with locomotives the arches were first strengthened by additional trussing in the parapets and, by the 1860s, wrought iron girders.

Whereas all of these bridges usually had masonry piers up to track level, and were thus composite structures, those on Brunel's West Cornwall Railway, opened in 1852, originally had timber piers instead. On the many viaducts of the later Cornwall Railway between Plymouth and Truro, opened in 1859, most of the piers were of stone up to 35 feet below track level. From the top of the piers, flaring timber braces supported the decking, though a few on the less stable creeks had to have all timber piers instead. Most of these viaducts had been replaced by the early 1900s, usually by building new ones alongside and diverting the track. In a few cases the stone sections of the piers of Brunel's originals still stand. The last of the timber bridges to carry passenger traffic was the College Wood viaduct on the Cornwall Railway's Falmouth branch, replaced in 1934.

Brunel was not the only engineer capable of building impressive bridges using timber as a major component in the design. In northern England, John and Benjamin Green were responsible for two fine bridges on the Newcastle & North Shields Railway, opened in 1839. The bridges at Willington and Ouseburn had stone piers supporting segmental ribbed arches of laminated timber and it was always intended to replace these with iron. This was duly carried out in 1869 and the new ironwork mirrored the timber it replaced. Two similar viaducts were built on Joseph Locke's Sheffield, Ashton-under-Lyne & Manchester Railway at Etherow and Dinting Vale in 1842 and 1844; although aesthetically attractive these were structurally less successful and the timbers were replaced by iron girders in 1859 and 1860. Etherow viaduct had three timber 38m wide arches and was the more elegant of the two when built, but the Dinting Vale viaduct was the larger, with masonry approach arches on either side of the five 38m wide timber ones. The arches sprang from canted set-backs in the tall Millstone Grit piers, and the infilled slots in which each of the parallel laminated arches of Baltic pine fitted are still visible. The replacement of the arches by wrought iron girders did little for their appearance, which was later completely ruined by the addition of additional brick piers by the Great Central Railway just after the First World War.

A rare example of a large all timber bridge in Scotland was that built by the Great North of Scotland Railway over the River Don at Inverury, opened in 1854 and consisting of ten openings, all on a skew to the single line of track carried. Later in the nineteenth century several minor bridges were built of timber in the far north of Scotland simply to save costs. Murdoch Paterson's simple timber trestle bridge at Aultnaslanach near Moy was on the Highland Railway and built in 1897. It is now the only timber bridge on a main line in Scotland.

Indeed, very few timber bridges of any size have survived to the end of the twentieth century. One notable exception is on the former Cambrian Railways coast line, crossing

39   *Landowners often insisted on special treatment when agreeing to allow railways to cross their land. This minor accommodation bridge on the disused northern section of the Severn Valley Railway, photographed in 1983, was built in 1861 and decorated as an eye-catcher from Apley Park on the opposite side of the river.*

the treacherous estuary of the Afon Mawddach immediately to the south of Barmouth. Barmouth Bridge, the longest ever built in Wales, is impressive for its length and durability rather than for its architectural merits. It was designed by the contractor, Thomas Savin, and virtually ready in the summer of 1866, though officially opened a year later. It is nearly half a mile long and had 121 spans in all, 113 of which were wooden, the remainder being a wrought-iron section at the north end originally including a cumbersome draw-bridge that was replaced by the present swing bridge. The change led to five wider spans replacing the eight original ones at this end of the bridge. In recent years the bridge has survived several attempts to close it, but its worst enemy was a vicious worm, the Teredo, that was found to have invested most of the timbers in 1980. Fortunately the bridge was repaired, at great expense, and reopened in the following year after temporary repairs, and fully repaired by 1986.

    Timber was, and sometimes still is, used in other ways in bridges, usually as decking. Commonly, timber balks are laid between the girders of metal bridges to support the ballast in which the sleepers sit, and, on overbridges, to support the roadway. On many station footbridges, timber is still used for the treads of the steps and for the handrails.

    What is often overlooked when studying the great masonry arches of railway bridges is the amount of timber and skilled carpentry needed in their construction, and without which they simply could not have been built. Apart from the obvious need to scaffold the abutments and piers as the masonry was built, the most difficult job was to create the temporary timber framework, or centring, for the arches. Only when the last of the voussoirs of the arch was securely in place could that centring be removed. Good quality timberwork became important again with the advent of concrete bridges, which required accurately set out shuttering. In many cases, the structure of the centring for masonry or for concrete could be both expensive and elaborate but because of its temporary nature seldom if ever survived. There may be scars in the masonry to show where some of the centring once went.

Stone & Brick

The oldest surviving railway bridges date to the eighteenth century and are mainly built of stone. This was a material that would have been well-known to local masons and the designs needed would have been little different to those they were used to building — the main difference being in underbridges the need to keep the track bed level. On many road bridges, the decking was deliberately sloped to a central peak to aid drainage and to fit in with the structural design of the bridge's arch.

The most famous early railway bridge of all is the Causey Arch, or Dawson's Bridge, built to carry a waggonway across the Beckley Burn near the village of Tanfield in County Durham. The double tracked 4ft gauge line belonged to the Grand Allies, a group of coal masters, and was opened in 1727. It was designed by a local mason, Ralph Wood, and consists of one single stone arch of three 'rings' springing from the bedrock on either side; the span of the arch is 102ft (over 30m) — still one of the largest built for any railway in Britain — and the height above the springing is 35ft (10m). Neither its width nor design would have been unusual for its date for a road bridge over a river, but to build on this scale for a railway certainly was. It is claimed to be the oldest surviving railway bridge in the world.

A far less well-known waggonway bridge survives at Newdale, now part of Telford, Shropshire, and was built around 1760. The Newdale complex of foundry and workers' housing was built by the famous Coalbrookdale Company — hence the name — but the foundry itself was very short-lived. The bridge carried a waggonway leading to the site over a small brook to the south-east and consists of two segmental brick arches with stone abutments and spandrels. The line probably did not last very long after the foundry closed, but the bridge, fortunately, did and was restored in 1987. Ironically, later in that same year the original Newdale foundry buildings were rediscovered, virtually unrecognisable within a run-down farm. Despite being immediately listed because of their importance — arguably being the most intact industrial buildings of their period in an area known as the Cradle of Industry and a World Heritage Site — the listing was overturned by the then government and they were flattened when the whole area was open-cast by British Coal.

From the late 1770s onwards the number of surviving waggonway and plateway bridges increased, as there were more and more lines being built. Two of the finest surviving examples are river bridges. In 1812 William Jessop designed a stone bridge to take the Kilmarnock & Troon line over the River Irvine at Gateshead; this has elegant rounded cutwaters between each of its four spans. In England, William James built a nine arched brick bridge over the River Avon in Stratford-upon-Avon to take the Stratford & Moreton Railway. This was probably finished in 1823, three years before the line was completely open; it had closed by the end of the century, its rails were lifted in 1918 to help the war

40   *The quality of details on early railway bridges was often exceptional. This is part of the fine rusticated stonework and dentilled cornice of the bridge carrying the tracks into the London & Birmingham Railway's original 1837 Birmingham station in Curzon Street. It does not cross a main road or important street, merely the short Digbeth branch canal.*

effort, and it is now a footbridge used by hundreds of thousands of tourists every year. Other examples of tramway bridges include those at Ticknall, Derbyshire on the Ticknall Tramway of 1802, built just like an ordinary road bridge in local stone with brick in the arch.

The beginning of steam railways led inevitably to far greater weights and to far greater demands on the bridge builders. This can be seen in George Stephenson's Sankey Viaduct on the original Liverpool & Manchester Railway, a structure both backward looking and pioneering. In structural and engineering terms it was fairly conventional, and certainly not revolutionary like Stephenson's earlier iron Gaunless Bridge (*q.v.*). However, in terms of scale it announced the arrival of the railway age.

The 200m long viaduct took the double tracked line across the valley of the Sankey Brook on nine 15m wide arches and was over 20m high. The core was built of brick but the whole structure was faced in stone. Between the arches there are thin pilasters and beneath them the piers are unusually splayed out for additional integral strength, giving the whole structure an air of solidity that was, presumably, deliberate. Nor was this simply an illusion as, remarkably, the viaduct is still in use by main line trains today making it the oldest of any size in use in the world. On the same line, Stephenson was capable of

41   Brunel's Wharncliffe viaduct at Hanwell, then outside London, carried the GWR over the Brent valley and was finished in 1838. This is the view from the south-east and the break between the original and the northern extension is fairly obvious.

designing much more elegant bridges, such as the splendidly detailed skew bridge by Rainhill station — a work of rusticated ashlared stone and elongated voussoirs combining engineering excellence and beauty.

The basic design of masonry railway bridges was set by the opening of the Liverpool & Manchester and little changed apart from scale. Within a surprisingly short time many other large viaducts had been built that overshadowed the one over the valley of the Sankey Brook. In 1836 the London & Greenwich Railway opened their line to London Bridge station. It was engineered by Colonel G. T. Landmann and though it passed through mostly open fields for nearly four miles it ran on a seemingly endless and relatively low viaduct built of London brick containing no less than 828 arches. Some were wider than others, generally where the viaduct crossed a road at an angle and skew arches were needed. The viaduct was just under 8m wide and generally over 6m high and suffered from slight settlement early on. It was, and still is, the longest viaduct in Britain and from the start the company tried to let the areas under the arches for shops, warehouses and — less successfully — housing.

On Brunel's Great Western main line there appear to have been similar attempts to use the Twerton viaduct on the edge of Bath for housing and shortly after it was built eleven two-room houses built into the arches were let to a Mr Wilkins for his workers. Although these still have traces of windows and doors they do not appear to have been inhabited subsequently. Brunel's finest viaduct on this line was at the other end, on the edge of London — the eight span brick-built Wharncliffe viaduct crossing the Brent valley at

42   *Henry Robertson's Chirk viaduct across the Cerriog valley, finished in 1848, literally overshadowed Telford's aqueduct, seen through the arches. The two arches at the right-hand end replaced an original timber one and there are subtle differences; those arches do not have keystones and the parapet does not have a dentilled cornice under it.*

Hanwell and opened in 1838. Its elegant proportions are partly the result of its splayed piers, which give it a vaguely Egyptian feel, and the shallow segmental arches. Built for two lines of broad gauge track, it was widened in the same style during the 1870s when two more standard gauge tracks were added on the north side; the construction break between the two builds is obvious.

John Urpeth Raistrick, who in his twenties had built the pioneering locomotive *Catch-me-who-can* in 1808, engineered two particularly fine brick viaducts in Sussex much later in his career. The first is probably the most famous, carrying the double tracks of the London & Brighton line over the valley of the Ouse near Balcombe on 37 arches of different heights up to 28m, and mainly of 9.1m span. The viaduct and abutments are a little under 440m in length. In Brighton itself, Raistrick designed the London Road viaduct carrying the line to Lewes which was opened in 1846. This shared many of the design features of the Ouse viaduct, including the tall cut-outs, topped and tailed by arches, through the piers that reduced the amount of bricks needed in them without compromising their strength. Although built of brick, both were elegantly decorated with moulded stone imposts and superb stone balustrading; the Ouse viaduct even has delicate Italianate pavilions flanking the track at either end. The masonry and pavilions are almost certainly the work of the line's architect, David Mocatta.

Other notable early masonry viaducts include Stockport viaduct (1842), Crimple viaduct, near Harrogate, North Yorkshire (1848); Chirk and Dee viaducts on the Shrewsbury & Chester Railway (1848); Whalley viaduct, Lancashire (1850, widened to

43   *The urban viaducts carrying lines through many larger towns were one of the less welcomed aspects of the railways, but are often major engineering achievements. Places such as Manchester and Huddersfield have notable examples, as does Birmingham; this brick viaduct is part of the former GWR's long approach to the city centre from the south.*

two tracks 1872); Welwyn viaduct, Hertfordshire, on the Great Northern Railway (1850); and Yarm viaduct, Yorkshire (1852). In northern Scotland there were some very fine masonry bridges built from the 1860s, mostly designed by Joseph Mitchell who had been involved in road building in the Highlands for many years. Some of his bridges, such as that over the Ness at Inverness on the Inverness & Ross-shire Railway of 1863, resemble road bridges and all are characterised by their elegance. The finest of his masonry bridges carried the single-line Inverness & Perth Junction Railway along the side of the Pass of Killiecrankie on a slight curve; 155m long, and decorated with battlements and turrets, it was finished in 1863. The longest masonry bridge in Scotland, at Culloden, with its 28 spans, took the single line Highland Railway over the River Findhorn; it was designed by Mitchell's assistant, Murdoch Patterson, and opened in 1898.

The longest British viaduct over a valley, as opposed to one built in a town to save money, was built by the Midland Railway on their Kettering to Melton Mowbray line in Rutland. Designed by John Underwood and opened to goods traffic in 1879 it is 1166m long and has 82 brick arches. It impresses by sheer size rather than beauty. The Midland Railway later built the well-known Dent Head, Ribblehead, and Arten Gill viaducts in the bleak moorlands on the route of their Settle to Carlisle line. These are famous not so much for their size — which is impressive enough — but for the fact that they were built

44.   *Joseph Mitchell, of the Inverness & Perth Junction, had to accommodate an existing road bridge over the River Garry under the railway bridge at Calvine, Tayside. He did so with some style. The line, a remarkable feat of engineering throughout, opened in 1863 and this photograph was taken before the line was doubled in the late 1890s when an ugly girder bridge was built alongside the old bridge.*

in the face of such adversity in such inhospitable terrain. They were designed by John Crossley and opened in 1875.

Building viaducts of relatively short spans over valleys became a relatively simple exercise. The number of arches was scarcely relevant, and heights up to 30m or more hardly troubled the engineering skills of the day. Once the piers were built the timber centring could be erected and the masonry arches built; after the mortar had set the centring was removed and the structure was virtually finished. The only real problems occurred where the soils on which they were built were unstable, and these could be resolved by piling or deep footings. Mistakes were made and natural disasters did happen — one of the more dramatic being on the Rother viaduct of the Manchester, Sheffield & Lincoln line in 1848; floods undermined one of the piers which then fell onto its neighbour which then caused a domino effect in which all the other piers were destroyed; four men were killed.

Crossing some rivers, however, could cause far more problems if masonry alone was to be used. The wider the span the more difficult the construction and the greater the reliance on the nature of the rock on which the footings are built. Nevertheless, the successful results usually produced far more pleasing structures than the often monotonous viaducts. One of the earliest and most attractive of the steam railway bridges, and one that tested brickwork to its limits and defied public scepticism, was Brunel's famous bridge on the Great Western's main line at Maidenhead.

To cross the Thames he was faced with having to build a relatively low bridge over a very wide river without impeding the traffic on it. A two arch design was produced, each of the main arches being semi-eliptical with a span of 39m but rising only just over 7.3m from the springing. Their shallow profile seemed incapable of taking the weight of the traffic and Brunel teased the public by leaving the wooden centring scaffold in after the line had opened — but with a small gap between the timber and the masonry. When the scaffolding collapsed in a flood the bridge stood firm despite the doom-mongers, and it has done now for well over 150 years carrying trains ten or more times the weight of even the longest of the original Broad gauge era.

Amongst the finer wider spanned bridges are the Victoria Bridge over the Wear, built by the little-remembered Durham Junction Railway in 1838; its four main spans vary in width between 30 and 49m — the latter claimed at the time to be the widest in the world. The most dramatic stone arched railway bridge is the Ballochmyle viaduct in Ayrshire, designed by John Miller to carry the long-windedly titled Glasgow, Paisley, Kilmarnock & Ayr Railway over the Water of Ayr. Of superbly ashlared stone, it took just two years to build, and was opened in 1848; its central span is over 55m and the bridge is just under 52m high. Still in use, for most of its existence it has been the largest masonry span on any railway bridge in the world and is now the tallest railway viaduct in Britain.

Until the later nineteenth century, stone was the more fashionable building material and wherever possible was used for the building, or at least the facing stones, of railway bridges of any pretension. Throughout much of the south-east of England, stone was, however, in short supply and thus relatively expensive. This accounts for the large number of impressive brick viaducts and bridges in the region. In the more utilitarian second half of the nineteenth century, a time when many of the less well-funded lines were being built, the engineering 'blue' brick became almost ubiquitous in all but the best stone-producing areas.

Iron & Steel

The use of iron in railway bridges has a surprisingly long history. The first significant use of iron in civil engineering was the construction of the famous iron bridge over the Severn at the site that now bears the name Ironbridge, in Shropshire — cast in 1779 and open for road traffic by 1781. As this was an area famous for pioneering new uses for its iron, including iron railway wheels, axles and rails, it is possible that some small iron railway bridges were built too but no traces have so far been discovered. In South Wales, two early iron plateway bridges do survive, both quite small but both believed to be *in situ*. The oldest is the Pont y Cafnau built to take a plateway and water supply to the Cyfartha Works in Merthyr Tydfil and probably designed by Watkin George. It has a span of 14.3m and consists of two parallel cast-iron A-frames taking an iron decking that incorporates the plateway track. The Robertstown tram bridge near Aberdare is another preserved cast-iron bridge, built for a plateway between the Aberdare Canal and the iron works at Hirwaun in 1811, carrying the line over the Afon Cynon.

45   *The cast-iron Robertstown tram bridge near Aberdare was built to carry a plateway linking the Aberdare Canal and the iron works at Hirwaun over the Afon Cynon. Its date, 1811, is cast into its parapet and it is the oldest dated iron railway bridge in the world.*

The first iron edge-railway bridge was a quite remarkable structure designed by George Stephenson for a branch of the Stockton & Darlington Railway as early as 1822. Built to cross the River Gaunless near West Aukland, County Durham, it was finished in 1823 but rebuilt in 1824-5 following storm damage. The bridge combined the principles of both the arch and of suspension and used both wrought and cast iron. The line it was on was worked by horses initially before steam locomotives arrived in the mid 1830s. In 1901 the then owner, the North Eastern Railway, replaced the bridge with a masonry structure but showed foresight in carefully dismantling the old one, which now stands outside the National Railway Museum in York — an early example of industrial heritage conservation.

Cast iron does not rust easily and is very strong in compression — that is it can take heavy weights directly loaded on it. As its name implies, it is cast, when molten, and this allowed it to be formed into the most elaborate of decorative patterns. Unfortunately it is also brittle and not very good in tension and in this respect is not dissimilar to masonry. Used in an arched rib it can be far lighter than a masonry structure and thus the footings and the abutments can be lighter too, saving on cost and time. Wrought iron, on the other hand, is a more utilitarian substance, stronger in tension, better able to resist bending and lateral pulls on it, but more prone to rusting. It also needs to be worked more in production, the raw material being constantly hammered or rolled in the foundry and the finished iron needing more effort in assembly, and it is more expensive to produce.

45   Joseph Mitchell was not only adept at masonry bridges. To get the Inverness & Aberdeen Junction across the Spey at Orton he used a type of wrought-iron box-girder bridge. It was finished shortly after the line was opened, in 1858, but replaced by a more mundane lattice-girder bridge in 1906.

Stephenson used cast-iron arches for some of his bridges on the London & Birmingham line, the best known of which is that at Denbigh Hall near Bletchley, where it crosses over the Roman Watling Street — the Holyhead Road. The line crosses on the skew but Stephenson ignored this and built instead a straight bridge over the road which obviously had to project either side of the railway crossing over it and which at first sight seemed to be a rather wasteful use of resources. However the headroom and width of one of the main roads in the country had to be retained and to build a cast iron arch on the skew in order to do this would have required much longer castings, which Stephenson seemed reluctant to use.

Ironically, the use of cast-iron received a set back in 1847 by the collapse of his new Dee bridge at Chester. This was a girder bridge, using cast-iron girders between stone piers and abutments on the Chester & Holyhead Railway. The brittle nature of cast-iron was shown all too clearly to be unsuitable to be used in girder form. As a passenger train passed over the bridge, one of the girders fractured and the carriages fell into the river resulting in the loss of five lives. Many cast-iron girder bridges had already been built and most would eventually be replaced, but other railway bridges of cast-iron arches were still built afterwards and cast iron would also continue to be used in cylinder or pillar form in composite iron structures.

Amongst the finest of the cast-iron arched railway bridges are three made by the Coalbrookdale Company which, like the famous iron bridge, cross the River Severn. The earliest is the Belvidere Bridge, carrying the Shrewsbury & Birmingham Railway across the river just to the east of Shrewsbury. Designed by William Baker it was opened in 1849 and each of its two arches have a span of just under 31m. Originally it had an elegant cast-iron balustrade but this was replaced by a more mundane affair when the bridge was restored in 1983.

The other two bridges are virtually identical and are both single spans designed by John Fowler. The earlier of the two, the Victoria Bridge at Arley, was single tracked and opened in 1862; it was built by the Severn Valley Railway and is fortunately on a part of that line now reopened as one of the finest preserved railways in the world. With a span of 61m, the main structure consists of four parallel cast-iron arches made up of bolted segments and trussed together by wrought iron ties. It was claimed to be the widest single span cast iron railway bridge in the world when finished. The almost identical Albert Edward bridge further upstream is not on the Severn Valley line but instead carried the 'Wenlock No.2 railway' of the Much Wenlock, Craven Arms & Coalbrookdale Railway across the river. Finished in 1864 it was slightly shorter than the Victoria bridge, but as it carried two lines of track instead of one the *Illustrated London News* were right in declaring that it was 'the largest cast-iron arch carrying a double line of railway that has yet been erected anywhere in the world.'

There are other particularly good examples of arched cast-iron bridges in the middle of towns, including the Friargate bridge that once carried the Great Northern Railway over Derby's finest Georgian street built as late as 1878. It is no longer in use by the railways but is still maintained. A similar bridge over the Foregate Street in Worcester is not quite what it seems, the decorative cast-iron work having no structural purpose; the bridge was remodelled in this way by the Great Western Railway in 1908.

Cast iron girders were often used in conjunction with masonry. Typically, the girders would be cast in I or upside down T shaped sections. Often these girders would have a cambered upper section and be taller in the centre to make up for the material's poor resistance to bending under heavy loads; this type of girder is described as being *hogged* or as *hogsbacked*. The girders would be laid parallel between the abutments and piers and either trussed together by wrought iron ties or physically linked by brick 'jack arches'. If jack arches were to be used, the lower flanges of the girders were usually sloped to hold the springing of the arches. The result was a strong structure suitable for both over and underbridges, and tens of thousands of such bridges, mostly for overbridges but a great many underbridges as well, still survive in daily use.

Wrought iron could be used, like cast, in girder or plate form but was structurally more adapt at coping with the stresses and strains created by heavy rail traffic. In many ways it could be used in the same way as timber, with relatively small pieces being joined together and trussed to form large integrated sections. Brunel's distrust of cast iron — 'a friable, treacherous, and uncertain metal' — had been compounded by the failure of his only major cast-iron bridge on the Great Western over Uxbridge Road in London in 1847 — the same years as the Dee Bridge disaster. Timber casing to the girders caught fire and they fractured. He did, however, see the benefits of using wrought iron and introduced one significant advance to using it in railway bridges.

In any arch, masonry, timber or iron, the loadings are transferred down the arch and

47   *One of the commonest forms of railway bridges was the wrought-iron (and later steel) girder bridge; this returning coal train from Buildwas Power Station, hauled by a Type 56 diesel locomotive, is passing under a typical girder overbridge near Madeley, Shropshire, in April 1983.*

into the abutments or piers. This puts a great deal of weight on the rest of the structure which therefore needs to be strong enough to take it. Land abutments can be as massive as necessary, but the intermediate piers on a multi-spanned bridge cannot. The time-old manner of reducing thrusts in wooden roof structures was by the use of a tie-beam across the building at the base of the roof. Typically this held the feet of the rafters together and by taking some of the loading on them produced a strong and virtually freestanding structure. Brunel used this basic trussing concept in his timber bridges and also realised the same thing could be achieved in iron.

A large iron arch could be tied at the springing level by a wrought iron tension tie and the assembly could then be virtually a self-contained structure with the tie taking much of the stress of the arch, allowing for larger single spans, slighter piers and abutments. The tie itself also supported the track bed, so that the arch was above it rather than being below it in the more traditional way, giving an additional bonus in the clearance below the bridge. Technically known as a *tied arch* or *bowstring arch*, this method proved immensely useful to the railway engineers.

Brunel's first bowstring bridge was on the branch line across the Thames into Windsor, opened in 1849 and still standing. Originally the three parallel bow-string arches of the 62m span were supported on concrete-filled cast-iron columns and the approach arches on one side of the river were of timber. The columns and the approach arches have been rebuilt in brick. The decking was originally of timber supported by wrought-iron cross-

48   *Brunel's pioneering and dramatic bow-string bridge carrying a GWR branch line across the Thames at Windsor was open to traffic in 1849 and despite some changes, is still in use. The original cast-iron piers and the timber approaches have been replaced in brick, but the triangular-sectioned arch ribs and most of the iron bracing is original (Ken Hoverd/Archive 1993).*

members; Brunel placed the balks of timber on his bridges on the diagonal to spread the load of passing trains onto as many cross-girders as possible. A year before the Windsor bridge was open Brunel's grand timber viaduct over the Usk at Monmouth on the South Wales Railway had burnt down; he replaced the central span with a second bowstring girder bridge.

One of the most spectacular bridges using the bowstring technique was also opened in 1849, Robert Stephenson's High Level bridge over the Tyne at Newcastle. It has six main spans 38m wide and the line is 36.5m above the normal water level. The arches of the bridge are of cast iron and the ties of wrought, matching the respective strengths of the different types of iron. The piers and approach arches are of superbly ashlared masonry. The railway is actually carried above the bowstring arches on a deck supported by cast iron, whilst at tie-beam level there is a road.

Wrought iron could also be used to make extremely long girders, either solid or latticed, flat or hogged, simply by bolting or riveting together sections of the metal until the desired length was reached. These techniques allowed the creation of long spans that could be supported on relatively thin masonry or iron piers. The two or more girders, flat or hog-backed, solid or latticed, would be laid between the abutments or piers and tied together by iron cross-ties and the decking added to support the track ballast. As with the bowstring bridges, the spans could be prefabricated away from site and simply lifted

49 Kew Bridge, across the Thames in west London, has clearly seen some alterations. Note how some of the piers are plainer than the others, presumably because they have replaced. It is a fairly typical example of a mid-Victorian lattice girder bridge, though more attractive than most, and was designed by W. R. Galbraith for the London & South Western Railway.

or rolled into place. Equally, when the line closed the ironwork could be taken away for scrap — leaving hundreds of beautifully built but redundant bridge piers and abutments up and down the country.

The most successful of these girders used for major bridges was the 'Warren Truss', first used in 1848 on the Bolton to Bury line. James Warren devised a latticed girder truss in which the top and bottom rails (the *chords*) are connected by a series of crossing diagonal braces some of which are in tension and some in compression giving the whole assembly a degree of self-support. A later variation on this is the Pratt or 'N' truss, in which the compression members between the chords are vertical and the tension members are single diagonals, giving the latticework the typical 'N' motif.

In 1830 the engineer of the famous Chain Pier at Brighton, Captain Samuel Brown, designed a suspension bridge to carry a branch of the Stockton & Darlington Railway over the River Tees near Stockton-on-Tees. It was not a success and was replaced in 1841. Only two other suspension railway bridges were built in Britain, but these were also two of the most spectacular. George Stephenson once put forward the idea of placing a line of railway on Telford's Menai Straight suspension bridge but this was, fortunately, abandoned. However the railway from Chester to Holyhead needed to cross the Straights, and at a level that would not impede shipping. Robert Stephenson had initially thought of a suspension bridge but had the idea of stiffening it by running the trains through iron

50   A maintenance train waits on the Matlock branch near Cromford in November 1987; the bridge over the Derwent is of Pratt truss design, with the track on the lower chords. The double line has obviously been singled and the deck details are quite clear.

tubes. The chains were subsequently abandoned when experiments by William Fairbairn and the mathematician Eaton Hodgkinson demonstrated that the tubes could be self-tensioning and needed no additional support. This did not stop the construction of the three central masonry towers, which were carried up to their designed level and pierced to take the suspension chains — presumably as a precaution in case they were needed after all. The Britannia Bridge opened in 1850 but was badly damaged by a fire caused by young trespassers in 1970. The tubes were subsequently replaced by a deck supported by steel arches and a roadway was added above the railway a few years later — creating a nice archaeological conundrum for industrial archaeologists a few centuries from now.

Before Stephenson's Britannia Bridge and its pioneering smaller cousin at Conwy were finished, Brunel had started on the Royal Albert Bridge to carry the Cornwall Railway over the River Tamar, the boundary between Devon and Cornwall. Tests of the strata under the river had been made in 1848 but then works stopped until 1853. This bridge also had to be a high bridge because of Admiralty restrictions and Brunel decided on having only two large main spans, each just under 140m wide. He used a novel combination of the tubular and suspension technology which overshadows the quality of the tall curving approach viaducts. The iron tubes in each span are curved up in arched form and balance the chains suspended from the masonry towers. The height of the bridge is reinforced by its narrowness; it was originally designed to take a double line of track but Brunel was forced to single it, and save £100,000 in the process. It was opened in 1859. Its dramatic lines have been compromised by the new roadbridge built immediately alongside.

Relatively few all iron bridges were built in Britain. The ones that were generally used cast-iron for the pier supports and wrought iron for the trussing, ties, and girders. Most of these were used to cross rivers, particularly in the late-1850s and 1860s, and were not particularly tall. In 1857 the double-tracked Crumlin viaduct, Gwent, over the Ebbw Valley was opened and seemed to take iron bridgework to the limit. This ten span bridge, over 500m long, was designed by T. W. Kennard (partner of the inventor of the Warren truss) for the Taff Vale Extension line of the Newport, Abergavenny & Hereford Railway. It took four years to build, cost £62,000, and looked a little like a timber trestle bridge. At its tallest point it was 61m high, making it the highest railway bridge ever built in Britain; the line closed in 1964 and the bridge dismantled in 1967 leaving only the stone abutments on either side.

The Crumlin viaduct was not widely copied, though the Warren trusses it used for its main girders were. Two similar bridges were built, and the experience of these led to the construction of the longest and most tragic railway bridge of all. Sir Thomas Bouch's name will always be tarnished by the failure of the Tay Bridge. Before then, Bouch had designed a tall and slender brick viaduct over the Hownes Gill in County Durham, opened in 1858 and still standing. When appointed to design the bridges on the South Durham & Lancashire Union Railway between Barnard Castle and Tebay, he used various designs, some of masonry, some of trussed iron girders on tall masonry piers, and two, at Deepdale and Belah, entirely of iron. These two tall bridges must have looked decidedly spindly in comparison to the stone viaducts and were clearly influenced by Kennard's earlier design. The viaduct at Belah, finished in 1861, was the largest, over a thousand feet long and, at nearly 60m above the river, the highest railway bridge in England. The line closed in 1962 and the iron viaducts were dismantled in the following year.

In the late 1870s Thomas Bouch was at the height of his fame and was building three spectacular bridges in eastern Scotland. The longest was over the Tay estuary for the North British Railway, linking the Kingdom of Fife at Wormit with the city of Dundee. At 3,160m long it was also the longest railway bridge in Europe. As the bridge was approaching completion a reporter from the *Illustrated London News* commented on 'the sense of enormous strength in the structure....' and on 'the excellent finish of every part'. It carried a single track 23.5m above high tide level on 86 wrought-iron lattice girder spans supported by cement filled cast-iron pillars rising from paired brick piers. The bridge was opened in June 1878 and Queen Victoria knighted Bouch after crossing the bridge on her way to Balmoral in the following summer.

Unfortunately a mixture of poor design and poor workmanship led to disaster at the end of 1879. For most of the length of the bridge the track ran on top of the latticed girders but over the main navigation channel it ran inside them — a section known as the 'High Girders'. Bouch had completely ignored the problems of wind pressure and on the 28th December a gale had blown up. A local train from Burntisland to Dundee left Wormit just after 7pm and as it entered the High Girders it seems that a particularly strong gust of wind hit the girders which collapsed and took the train as well. None of the 75 people on board

51   *An LNER semi-fast passenger train crosses the Forth Bridge in the late 1930s and is dwarfed by its sheer size. The bridge, opened in 1890, is still one of the engineering wonders of the world.*

survived. Bouch's reputation and health were also destroyed and he died less than a year later. A similar design of wrought-iron bridge across the South Esk to the north-east at Montrose by Bouch was almost finished by then but after testing was demolished without being used. His grandest scheme of all, a suspension bridge to carry the main line over the Firth of Forth, was also abandoned; the only relic is the base of the central pier — planned to be 183m high — on the island of Inch Garvie which later supported a lighthouse.

The new Tay Bridge was designed by William Henry Barlow and built by William Arrol. Arrol had also rebuilt the bridge over the South Esk — traditionally seen as the prototype for the new Tay Bridge. Much of the ironwork was reused from the old Tay Bridge but the old piles were condemned and the new bridge had to built immediately upstream. After much dispute, the old brick piers were allowed to remain and now poke their heads eerily above the waters of the firth. The main supports of the new bridge were again of cast-iron pillars on brick piers, whilst the girders were of wrought iron and the decking was of mild steel; altogether 10 million bricks, 19,000 tons of wrought iron, 3,500 tons of steel, 2,500 tons of cast iron and three million rivets were used in its construction. The far more substantial girder bridge took two lines of track and opened in 1887. It was actually a little longer than the old bridge, at 3264m long, and is still the longest in Europe. The local self-style poet Laureate, William McGonagal was moved to verse, praising the bridge and reassuring others of its strength in his inimitable way:

> Beautiful new railway bridge of the silvery Tay
> With your strong brick piers and buttresses in so grand array
> And your thirteen central girders, which seem to my eye
> Strong enough all windy storms to defy....

Whilst the girders still the storms defy, it cannot be called the most beautiful of bridges. Indeed, Dundee, which has one of the finest natural settings of any major city, is ill served by the designs of both of its bridges; the railway bridge is utilitarian and the 1960s road bridge is ordinary. This is in direct contrast to the Firth of Forth to the south which possesses one of the finest pairs of bridges in the world.

Of these the most famous, and the only one actually still called the Forth Bridge (as opposed to the Forth rail bridge) was designed by John Fowler and Benjamin Baker and was again built by William Arrol. It made use of the recently proven mild steel in all but the granite piers of the approaches and tower bases. Apart from the approaches, it consists of three huge towers of steel tubes 110m high linked by cantilevered latticed girder spans 521m wide. It cost three million pounds, a fabulous amount of money for its time, but since it opened in 1890 it has rightly been considered to be one of the world's engineering masterpieces.

The introduction of the Bessemer process meant that the quality and cost of steel production respectively increased and decreased in the late 1870s. Mild steel has most of the benefits of both cast and wrought iron without their inherent defects and became the standard material for girder bridges of all kind from the start of the twentieth century. Another major advance from the 1940s has been the use of welding instead of riveting in the joining of steel plate and trussed girders.

1   A 'Sprinter' unit heads through the Shropshire hills on a Manchester-Cardiff trip in 1987. The line is
     now such a part of the scenery it is often difficult to realise the impact that it would originally have had.

2   Beautifully restored Stanier 2-8-0 No.8233 passes the unrestored cab of a dismantled locomotive at
     Kidderminster, Worcestershire, on the Severn Valley Railway. Few of the original parts of either will have
     survived. (1987)

3   *Preserved railways come in all shapes and sizes and some of the earliest were the narrow gauge lines of Wales. This train is on the Welshpool & Llanfair Light Railway in Powys, a 2ft 6in gauge line opened in 1903 and closed in 1956. In July 1982* Joan, *an 0-6-2T of 1927, heads a passenger train of carriages from Austria and Sierra Leone.*

4   *A narrow-gauge plateway wagon at the restored flint mill in Cheddleton, North Staffordshire. Such internal systems were vital for many industries but were often very lightly constructed and have left few traces.*

5   *A typical abandoned railway cutting, though in this case it has been partly reused as a farm track. For this reason some drainage has at least been kept working. This is on the former Bishop's Castle Railway, opened in 1866 and closed as long ago as 1936.*

6   *Not all lines were expensively built, especially those built under the Light Railways Act of 1896. In 1985 this horse was grazing on the trackbed of the Cleobury Mortimer & Ditton Priors Light Railway opened in 1908; beyond it is one of the original wooden station buildings. Elsewhere along the line, embankments have been ploughed out.*

7   Ventilation shafts are usually the only evidence that there is a tunnel below. The two towers over the
    'great shafts' of Robert Stephenson's Kilsby tunnel, Northants., on the London & Birmingham are
    bigger than most. The one in the distance is more typical. Undulations of the ground are the result of the
    spoil tipping during construction.

8   A 'Sprinter' unit leaves the original bore of the Dinmore tunnel in Herefordshire on the former
    Shrewsbury & Hereford Railway heading south in 1989. Opened in 1853 with a single bore, a second
    was soon needed and built at a slightly higher level.

9 *The small two-arch bridge of stone and brick once carried a waggonway to Newdale across the stream and was built around 1760. The new works at Newdale, Shropshire, were not a success, but it is unclear when the waggonway closed. This photograph was taken shortly after the bridge was restored in 1986-7.*

10 *This underbridge beneath the former Coalport branch of the L&NWR in modern-day Telford seems too narrow to cross a road and too high and wide for a simple footpath. It was, instead, built for a horse-drawn plateway, which when the bridge was built in 1861, was still an important part of the local transport infrastructure.*

11   *George Stephenson's Gaunless Bridge seems suprisingly modern in appearance but was first erected on the Stockton & Darlington Railway in 1823-5. In 1901 it was saved by the North Eastern Railway and dismantled; it has since been re-erected outside the new National Railway Museum in York.*

12   *A monument to the Railway Mania of the 1840s — the fine viaduct across the Wharfe at Tadcaster, Yorkshire, built for George Hudson's York & North Midlands Railway as part of a new direct route between York and Leeds but abandoned in 1849.*

13 *Barmouth bridge, Gwynedd, from the south, the longest in Wales and the longest wooden bridge in Britain. Designed and built by Thomas Savin for the Cambrian Railways, it opened in 1867. It was repaired, at great expense, by British Rail in the 1980s.*

14 *An overbridge on the central Wales line near Knighton, Powys; at this point the road runs alongside the railway and to cross over the bridge traffic has to climb the long approach embankments and negotiate two sharp bends, The decorated parapet is of cast iron; the line opened in 1864. (1999)*

15   *Ex-GWR 4-6-0 No.6960* Raveningham Hall *crosses a simple cast-iron girder underbridge south of Eardington on the Severn Valley Railway in 1984. The casting on the girder shows where and when it was made.*

16   *A typical overbridge of brick arch and stone abutments. This carried a main road over the projected Welsh main line section of the Potteries, Shrewbury & North Wales Railway at Pontryhdmeredydd, Powys, and was clearly designed to take double-tracks. It was built about 1866.*

17   *Not the tower of a border castle, but part of the Knucklas viaduct on the Central Wales line opened in 1864 which carries it across the Heyope Valley just to the west of Knighton, Powys.*

18   *Death throes of a great station; by 1981 Broad Street, once one of the busiest of London's terminii, was shockingly run down and unkempt. Opened by the North London Railway in 1865, it finally closed in 1986.*

19   *Arley station, Worcestershire, on the preserved Severn Valley Railway, probably never looked as good as it does now; it is typical of the plainer stations built from the 1860s onwards. This view of 1984 is one that will scarcely change again.*

20   *The world's first proper railway station, Liverpool Road, Manchester, opened in 1830. The brick building on the left predates the railway; the station proper is to the right and seems to be just another town house. This view, in typical Manchester weather, was taken in 1988.*

21   *Gobowen's fine Italianate station on the former Shrewsbury & Chester Railway opened in 1848 and was designed by Thomas Penson. Recently it had been allowed to become rather shabby but local initiatives, especially by a local girls' school, led to its splendid restoration.*

22   *The picturesque station seen to perfection; this is the station at Berwyn in the Dee Valley, Clwyd, closed in 1964. This shot was taken in 1981, since when the station has been reopened by the ambitious Llangollen Railway Society.*

23   *The original Shrewsbury & Birmingham terminus in Wolverhampton was approached through a separate gateway in Queen's Street. After many years of neglect it has been restored as part of a bus station. Work is in progress in this view of 1988.*

24   *Finding a use for a disused station in large towns can be difficult. This is the now redundant Moor Street station built by the Great Western in the heart of Birmingham to cater for commuters. The rare example of a virtually unaltered Edwardian terminus urgently needs to be protected.*

25   *A detail of the decorative ironwork in the roof of Thomas Prosser's new York station of 1877.*

26 A detail of the restored cast and wrought-iron capitals of the canopy at Great Malvern station, Worcestershire. The buildings, completed in 1862 for the Worcester & Hereford Railway, were designed by E W Elmslie.

27 The Great Eastern signal box at Broad Street station, London, in 1981, a few years before it closed. Even at this date, the GER pattern long-armed semaphore signal looked a little old-fashioned on an all-electric line.

28   *Coton Hill goods yard in Shrewsbury, empty and snowbound in 1985. Once busy goods and marshalling yards have largely disappeared because of road competition, the effective ending of 'pick-up' and waggon-load goods traffic, and the introduction of 'train-load' and 'merry-go-round' trains.*

29   *The Cambrian Railways were formed by the amalgamation of several Welsh companies but had their headquarters in Oswestry, just over the English border. The large works were capable of everything from building locomotives to repairing goods waggons and, though closed in the late 1960s, are one of the least altered and best preserved in the country.*

30   Crossing keeper's cottages were needed when gates were operated manually day and night, but the spread
      of signal boxes meant that most were not really needed long before the introduction of automatic barriers.
      The cottages tended to still be used by railway workers. This one is on the former Shrewsbury & Chester
      line at Whittington, opened in 1848, and the design matches the nearby station.

31(left)   Rail reused as a quarter-mile post on a former Cambrian Railways line.
32(right)   Concrete gradient post on a line near Brownhills, West Midlands.

52   *Stephenson's Britannia Bridge over the Menai Straits was badly damaged by fire in 1970. Only the masonry towers, of Runcorn sandstone encased in Anglesey limestone, survive of the tubular bridge and were reused as the piers for a new steel arched bridge that carries both rail and road. Work is shown in progress in this photograph of 1971 (BR – London Midland Region).*

Once an iron bridge became redundant, its girders and piers were usually dismantled and sold for scrap. Thousands of bridges were treated in this way in the wholesale line closures of the 1960s. All that usually remains are the masonry abutments, with just the fixing slots in them to show where the girders went, and the adjacent earthworks. Even the great iron viaducts at Crumlin and Belah have left little trace, other than some odd terraces on the valley sides where the ground was levelled for their piers.

Concrete

The use of structural concrete was developed during the latter part of the nineteenth century and amongst its pioneers was 'Concrete Bob' McAlpine, founder of Robert McAlpine & Sons. He gained the contract for the construction of the West Highland Railway extension from Fort William to Mallaig, opened in 1901. Naturally he saw concrete as an ideal medium for the bridges and viaducts on the difficult route through remote, and spectacular, scenery. Timber shuttering was erected and the concrete simply poured in to it. The design of the viaducts was little different than the masonry arches of

53   *The curving viaduct in this c.1950s photograph is made not of stone, but concrete. It is the Glenfinnan viaduct, built by 'Concrete Bob' McAlpine for the West Highland Railway in 1901.*

half a century earlier, but the visual differences between weathered locally quarried stone and virtually indestructible concrete are marked. Nevertheless, at least this line was spared the use of the by then almost ubiquitous engineering brick and latticed girders, and several of the viaducts on the line, such as the curving Glenfinnan Viaduct, 380m long and 30.5m high, do have a charm all of their own. This had 21 arches of 15m span, which were not technically too difficult to build. However, the single-arched Borrowdale Bridge, with its 38.8m span, on the Arisaig estate was for several years the widest concrete bridge in the world.

At the opposite end of Britain, concrete was used in a completely different way for a bridge over the Tamar built by the Bere Alston & Calstock Light Railway in 1908. The 12 span 36.5m high bridge was constructed in concrete blocks and erected in much the same way as a normal stone bridge. It was designed by Messrs. Galbraith & Church.

The first use of reinforced concrete, as opposed to cast or blocks, on a main line was probably the bridge on the Avonmouth Docks to Filton line across an accommodation road at Hallen. It was opened in 1907 and used the Hennebique system of construction. In recent years there have been several pre-stressed concrete bridges built on the railways, usually replacing older ones when lines are electrified or built as the result of new roads or motorways. Two purely railway inspired structures of concrete were built in the early 1960s on the London-Birmingham main line — flyovers at Rugby and Bletchley.

8 Tunnels

The point at which a broad overbridge becomes a short tunnel is a moot one, but officially, a tunnel is now considered to be cut into the natural rock. This does not then include the very many 'man-made' tunnels in which cuttings have been dug and then roofed over — a process known as 'cut and cover'. In the early days of steam railways, opponents claimed that allowing passenger trains through tunnels was tantamount to torture, placing them at the risk of asphyxiation, mental distress, or deafness. Even in the supposed calm of a Parliamentary committee room when the Great Western Railway's bill was being discussed in 1834, it was claimed that the tunnel was 'monstrous and extraordinary' and that 'The noise of two trains passing in a tunnel would shake the nerves of this assembly. I do not know such a noise. No passenger would be induced to go twice.'

With tunnels, as with many other things, the railways borrowed heavily from the experiences of the canal builders of the late eighteenth and early nineteenth century. The canal builders had, in turn, learnt from the miners and one of the earliest 'proper' canals — the Bridgewater — had ended in mine workings. By the start of the nineteenth century there were several astonishing tunnels on the canal system, including Harecastle (2649m long), Sapperton (3482m long), and the longest, Standedge (5210m long).

Excluding any underground rails in mine workings, and elongated bridges under roads such as that on the Alloa Waggonway of 1766, the earliest known railway tunnel in the world is generally considered to be on the Peak Forest Tramway at Chapel Milton, Derbyshire, opened in 1796. This is about 80m long and has a simple horse-shoe section with plain stone portals at either end and was presumably designed by the line's engineer, Benjamin Outram. The longest recorded tramway tunnel was the Pwll-du Tunnel near Blaenavon, Gwent, cut through older mine working by its engineer and owner, Thomas Hill, and opened in 1825; it was just under 2000m long. The sophisticated engineering principles used are not too surprising as by this time some of the great canal tunnels had already been built.

Some of these early tunnels could be converted for use by the steam railways. Two of the best examples of this were the 281m long tunnel on the Ticknall Tramway at Ashby-de-la-Zouch, Leicestershire of c.1805, widened and converted to a standard gauge tunnel by the Midland Railway in 1874, and the Haie Hill tunnel on the Bullo Pill Railway (later the Forest of Dean Tramroad) in Gloucestershire. This was 972m long but only 2.5m or so high when it opened in 1809; it was converted by Brunel in 1854 to take the Broad gauge Forest of Dean branch of the South Wales Railway and subsequently altered again, this time to Standard gauge, in 1872. The Grosmont tunnel on the horse-drawn Whitby & Pickering Railway of 1836, on the other hand, proved too small to be adapted for locomotive haulage. The castellated portal of George Stephenson's first tunnel is dwarfed by that of the 1847 tunnel built by the York & North Midland Railway alongside it.

Three other substantial tunnels built before 1830 were eventually to take railway traffic but had not been designed for the purpose. Two had been cut through the chalk bluff between Higham and Strood to take the wide Thames & Medway Canal, opened in 1824 to save barges having to go around the Isle of Grain. The tunnels were 1400m and 2130m long with just a 50m gap between. In 1845 the South Eastern Railway began operating two tracks through the tunnels, one on the towpath, the other on timber decking built over part of the canal; in the following year the canal was infilled and proper tracks were laid. The line became part of their North Kent main line.

In London, Marc Brunel had started work in 1825 on a pedestrian tunnel under the Thames between Rotherhithe and Wapping. His more famous son, Isambard, was officially made Resident Engineer in 1827. After many setbacks and delays the two parallel bores were finally opened in 1843 but it was not a great commercial success. In 1869 it reopened as a railway tunnel — the first to go under water in the world — carrying the double tracks of the East London Railway. It is now part of the London Underground system. The engineer in charge of the rebuilding was Sir John Hawkshaw, who later achieved far greater fame when he designed the much longer Severn Tunnel.

Although the first major tunnel built to be used by a steam railway was, almost inevitably, designed by one of the Stephensons, it was not by George for the Liverpool & Manchester Railway, but by Robert, with the help of two of his father's then assistants, Joseph Locke and John Dixon, for the short Canterbury & Whitstable Railway. This opened to passengers in May 1830 and the tunnel, under Tyler Hill, was 757m long. Passenger traffic ended 101 years after the line opened, and goods traffic, in 1952.

On the Liverpool and Manchester Railway, which opened shortly after the Canterbury & Whitstable, George Stephenson built two tunnels. Both were at the Liverpool end and approached from the Olive Mount cutting in Edge Hill. The shorter, a little over 265m long, was on the route to the original passenger terminus on Crown Street and, to relieve any fears the passengers might have, it was lit by gas. The longer tunnel took the goods-only double-tracked and rope-hauled incline from the cutting down to the riverside docks at Wapping. It was 2026m long on a steady gradient of 1 in 48 and was just over 8.2m wide and just under 5m high. Work on the tunnel started from either end but when Stephenson's former assistant, Joseph Locke, checked the survey, he discovered that these two headings would miss each other — an observation that Stephenson did not take very well by all accounts and one that fuelled the rivalry between these two eminent railway engineers.

The occasional directness of both George and Robert Stephenson's route making and, more importantly, their desire to avoid any significant gradients, inevitably led to the creation of long and expensive tunnels. Robert Stephenson designed the first railway tunnel over a mile in length used by passengers. This was at Glenfield on the Leicester & Swannington Railway, opened in July 1832, and was 1597m long; passenger traffic stopped in 1928 and the line was closed in 1966.

Tunnels were generally cheaper to construct than very deep cuttings. They had the added advantage of not disturbing the ground above too much. This allowed it to be used for the same purposes for which it was used before the advent of the railway once the tunnel was complete, cutting down on the additional costs the railway company may have had in buying it and generally placating landowners and farmers by not dividing up their estates.

The manner of their construction depended on the nature of the rock through which they were cut. If the rock was uniformly solid and strong, then the tunnels could be made without even being lined. However, if the rock was soft or flawed, then lining was essential and additional strength was provided by creating an *invert arch* below the tracks. The worst material to tunnel through was soft clay, which often needed very expensive lining in the best engineering brick. In many tunnels the original optimism of the engineer about the strength of the native rock proved unfounded and the tunnel would have to be lined later. The nature of the rock also determined the manner in which it was physically dug, and the extent to which explosives would be needed.

Most tunnels of any length were started at both ends simultaneously. Shorter ones, up to a few hundred yards, could be finished in this way but longer ones usually required intermediate shafts. These were dug down along the route of the tunnel to the proposed track bed level and work could start from either side of the shaft. In this way there were many separate work faces on the tunnel in use at the same time, speeding up the construction providing there were enough workers available. The shafts were often quite substantial works in their own right, usually being brick-lined — for stability — as they were sunk. At the head would be a horse gin or, in some cases, a stationary steam engine to haul spoil up the shaft and out of the way. The shafts had the added benefit of providing ventilation and daylight to the workings.

In some cases where the terrain was suitable it was also possible to cut temporary horizontal side tunnels, or cross-cuts, at track level through the flank of a hill and to take spoil away from the main workings on temporary tramways laid within them. This was the case, for example, on the tunnels excavated by the South Eastern Railway through the edge of the cliffs between Folkestone and Dover.

Despite being protected from rainfall, it was even more important in tunnels to ensure that there was good drainage. Inevitably, the tunnel would cut through several natural springs and groundwater would also arrive at the tunnel through the rock. Good culverts were needed to take away the water to avoid damage to the ballast and sleepers and the brick lining. One particularly wet tunnel near Wakefield, Yorkshire, was originally given an internal lining of lead, but that was very unusual — and expensive.

Not all tunnels were deep tunnels, driven through the rocks far below the surface. Another type is formed by firstly creating a deep cutting, and then roofing it over. The technique of *cut and cover* was generally used in urban areas but was sometimes applied when a particularly stubborn or sensitive landowner insisted on the railway being hidden from his sight. Such tunnels predating the advent of the steam railway. The Ticknall Tramroad of 1803 passed Calke Abbey too close for comfort for Sir Henry Harpur who insisted on a tunnel 140m long to take the line under his main drive. As a result, the line, which had just crossed the main road on a bridge to the north, had to turn sharply on a

54   *The construction of tunnels was a massive undertaking often taking several years. J. C. Bourne produced fine series of watercolours showing the construction of early main lines. This is his view of the surface equipment of one of the 'great shafts' of Stephenson's Kilsby Tunnel, Northamptonshire.*

fairly steep descent to enter the tunnel, which survives. For some reason a second, shorter, tunnel was built further to the south — even though there was no drive and where, for the most part, the tramway ran in a shallow cutting. The cut-and-cover method of tunnelling was used for both tunnels.

At the start of the 1860s the Midland Railway had particular trouble with major landowners on their cross-Pennine line from Derbyshire to Manchester. The refusal of the Duke of Devonshire to allow the line through his estates led to the diversion of the proposed route which went close to Haddon Hall, home of the Duke of Rutland. He then insisted on a tunnel to take the line past the house without ruining his views. The Haddon tunnel was built as a result, and was just under 1000m long; part was actually bored out and the rest was created by the cut-and-cover method. Despite being such a shallow tunnel, part of it still collapsed during construction in 1861 and five men were killed.

The first of the great main line railway tunnels were on Robert Stephenson's London & Birmingham line. Those at Primrose Hill, London (1064m) and at Watford (1646m) were substantial works but both were overshadowed by the one at Kilsby on the northern tip of Northamptonshire which, at 2194m long, was easily the longest railway tunnel in the world when it was finished. When the first trial shafts were sunk the rock seemed to be oolitic limestone and no real difficulties were forecast. However, once work began it was soon realised that there were clay strata and quicksands — and a tremendous volume of water. Work was started from either end and from sixteen shafts but became flooded almost continuously. The contractor, James Nowell, literally took to his bed and died.

Robert Stephenson took over using direct labour. To cope he had thirteen steam-powered pumping engines, some of 160 horse power, built on the line of the tunnel working non-stop for almost two years extracting water at nearly 2000 gallons (9092 litres) a minute. Finally the workings were dry and the tunnel was ready for opening in 1838. The tunnel had consumed 36 million engineering bricks in its lining, portals and shafts and had cost over three times its original estimated price of £99,000. To cater for the fears that passengers would be suffocated, the tunnel was made higher than necessary and two of the ventilation shafts were 18m in diameter. These two 'great shafts' were topped by great crenelated brick towers, whereas the other access shafts are topped by utilitarian brick turrets. However, neither portal, even the one at the northern end visible from the main road, is particularly rich in decoration.

Kilsby was only the longest railway tunnel in the world for just three years. Whilst Stephenson was engaged on it, his friend and rival Brunel was working on his own major tunnel at Box, just east of Bath, which, when it was finished in 1841, was some 2937m long. The tunnel was on one of the three steeper sections of the otherwise virtually level Great Western Railway's main line, the gradient being in the order of 1:100. This in itself led to claims that trains in the tunnel whose brakes failed could rush out at the lower end travelling well over 100 miles an hour.

Work started in November 1836 on the 7.6m diameter shafts, between 21m and 91m deep, that needed to be sunk to tunnel level; six of which were subsequently retained for ventilation. The tunnel took the line through a few hundred metres of good quality Bath freestone, but much of the rest was subject to water problems. In November 1837 the workings were so badly flooded that they could not be restarted until the following summer. Again steam engines were introduced to help and eventually, after five years of work, the tunnel was finished but at far greater expense than planned and with the loss of many lives. Nearly a quarter of a million cubic yards of material, mostly Bath stone and Fullers' Earth, were excavated from the workings. The quality of the freestone in the tunnel and approach cuttings meant that much of it could be used for bridges on the line and also to decorate company buildings. Despite the freestone, most of the tunnel was lined using around thirty million locally made bricks. It is now clear that the tradition, first 'discovered' by the Daily Telegraph in 1859, that the sun shines directly through the tunnel on Brunel's birthday, is not true.

Box was an engineering triumph but Brunel was not always as successful. At Sapperton, on the line from Swindon to Cheltenham, his original deep tunnel was abandoned because of geological and financial difficulties and the route was altered to a higher level and shorter tunnels substituted. Abandoning unfinished tunnels was not unique to Brunel. When the Shrewsbury & Welshpool line was being built in 1860, the original contractor was forced to resign after experiencing problems with the tunnel at Middletown. The company secretary, Richard Samuel France, took over, abandoned the tunnel completely, rerouted the line, and thus began his own rather eccentric career in local railway affairs.

55   Bourne also drew the west portal of Brunel's Box tunnel on the Great Western main line to the east of Bath. This was designed in a loose classical style rather than the company's usual 'engineer's Gothic'.

Box remained the longest railway tunnel for longer than Kilsby had done, but a longer one still had already been started before it was open. The route of the Sheffield, Ashton-under-Lyne & Manchester Railway was originally planned by Charles Vignolles and it passed under the Pennines between Woodhead and Dunford Bridge. Here, at the summit of the line, 473m above sea level, a tunnel just over three miles long was planned on a gradient of 1 in 201. Originally designed for two lines of track, it was decided to cut costs and build it for just one. Vignolles had difficulties with the tunnel and was replaced by another of the great railway engineers of the day, Joseph Locke — a man who, ironically, avoided tunnels on his routes wherever possible. It was to be the first of several major tunnels through the Pennines. Although work started in October 1838, the first year was mainly taken up by the creation of camps for the workers and an access road in what was then a fairly remote part of England. Most of the accommodation at Woodhead was still almost prehistoric, many of the men living in crudely thatched drystone walled hovels.

Living and working conditions for the navvies were so atrocious, even by the standards of the day, that they led to a Government inquiry. The lack of care for them by the company was summed up by one of the engineers who told a Parliamentary committee that, because safety fuses for explosives took longer to set, he 'would not recommend the loss of time for the sake of all the extra lives it would save'. Despite the length of the tunnel, only five shafts were dug down to the track level, and one of these took over four years to be sunk because of problems with water seepage. By the time the tunnel, described as 'a wonderous triumph of art over nature' was opened to traffic at the end of 1845, 272,685 cubic yards (208,494 cu m) of material had been removed, 157 tons of explosives had been used, over £200,000 had been spent, hundreds of the navvies had been injured, and 33 men had lost their lives.

Inevitably the single bore proved a false economy and in 1847 work started on a second one alongside. Instead of sinking shafts down to the new line, 25 short crosscut tunnels were built from the original one. Despite a cholera epidemic, during which all the workers quite sensibly ran away, the new tunnel was finished in 1851. The inadequate ventilation and the narrow bores of the Woodhead tunnels made life very unpleasant for passengers, very dangerous for train crews, and virtually impossible for the signalmen working the understandably short-lived signal box placed in one of the crosscut tunnels at the start of the twentieth century. Matters did not improve until after the Second World War. Delayed plans to electrify the route were then restarted but neither tunnel proved capable of being upgraded. A new double-tracked tunnel was built to the south of the older bores between 1949 and 1953; the tunnel opened throughout in the following June. Smoke-free, lined in Portland cement, and lit by electricity it was a huge improvement on the old ones, but sadly short lived. Passenger services were withdrawn in 1970 and the last goods train ran in 1981. One of the oddest legacies ever of railway construction must have been the small sewage works at Dunham, built to serve the temporary workmens' village and left afterwards to serve the hamlet.

The first Woodhead's reign as the longest tunnel had been short-lived, being supplanted by the Standedge Tunnel on the Huddersfield & Manchester Railway. This was engineered by the otherwise little-known Alfred Lee, who had worked under Locke at Woodhead. Work started in February 1846 and was finished less than three years later, in January 1849. This remarkably short period for a tunnel 3 miles and 62 yards (4.9km) long was due to the existence of an earlier tunnel running almost parallel to it. The first Standedge tunnel was on the Huddersfield Canal, opened in 1811. Lee was able to dispense with most of the shafts that he would otherwise have needed for the new tunnel by simply creating a series of crosscut to the canal, some 50ft away. The main tunnel could be built from the cross-cuts and the spoil could be removed by canal barges. As at Woodhead, only a single line tunnel had been built and a second tunnel was opened in 1870. A third railway tunnel, this time for a double line of rails, was opened by the London & North Western company in 1894 and the two older ones are no longer used. The later Standedge tunnel has the unusual distinction of being the only one to be fitted with water troughs; it was the only long section of level track on the route.

Standedge remained the world's longest railway tunnel for several decades until 1871, being superseded by the Fréjus tunnel under the Alps between France and Italy. In Britain it was superseded by the construction of the Severn Tunnel between England and Wales. This was also the first major tunnel under an estuary; the first tunnel specifically designed to take a railway under a river was in London. Whereas Marc Brunel's Thames Tunnel had been designed for pedestrians and later converted to railway use, the Tower Subway was built for a railway and converted to pedestrian use. The cable-hauled train service opened, on a 2ft 6in gauge track, in the summer of 1870 and closed at the end of the year. After that it was used by pedestrians until 1896; for many years it was used to carry a water main under the Thames but is now redundant.

The Severn Tunnel was designed by Sir John Hawkshaw, is 4 miles 628 yards (7km) long, and was built between 1874 and 1886. Hawkshaw was also involved in one of the several failed attempts to build a tunnel under the Channel between England and France in the early 1880s. Another serious attempt in the early 1970s also failed but the scheme was again revived in the 1980s finally opening — hopelessly over budget and behind time — in 1994.

By their subterranean nature tunnels leave few traces on the surface, and these are generally limited to portals, air vents, and spoil heaps. Portals, virtually unnoticed by the passengers on the trains, could be elaborate or plain according to the whims of the railway companies that built them — or the wishes of the landowners through whose land they were built. Both the Stephensons and Brunel preferred bold castelated Gothic decoration where decoration was needed, the portals of the Robert Stephenson's Kilsby and Linslade tunnels on the London & Birmingham being typical. One contemporary thought these to be 'of far too elaborate design'. Robert's father had built similar portals at the narrow Grosmont tunnel and at Clay Cross tunnel on the North Midland Railway of 1840.

Other particularly fine castellated portals include James Raistrick's Clayton tunnel on the London & Brighton line of 1841, which has a cottage between the two octagonal towers of its north portal; Joseph Mitchell's Killiecrankie tunnel of 1863 on the Inverness & Perth Junction line; and, arguably the finest, the asymmetric north portal of Bramhope tunnel on the Leeds & Thirsk railway by Thomas Grainger, opened in 1849. The 23 men who died excavating that tunnel, over two miles long, are commemorated by a stone model of the north portal in Otley churchyard.

All engineers had to occasionally alter their tastes to suite local tastes. On the London & Birmingham Railway, the south portal of Stephenson's tunnel Primrose Hill tunnel in London's northern suburbs was treated in an Italianate style. His Trent Valley Railway, opened in 1847, passed through the Shughborough estate of the Earl of Lichfield, a landscape already dotted with follies by the Earl's predecessors. The railway company employed the architect J. W. Livock to design an ornate classical underbridge over one of the drives and grand portals — one like a Norman castle, the other vaguely Egyptian — to the half mile long tunnel.

On the Great Western Railway's main line the east end of the Brunel's Box tunnel, apart from simple stonework and rusticated voussoirs and pilasters, was virtually unadorned as it would not be seen from any highway. The west end, on the other hand, was only a few yards from the main London to Bristol turnpike road and so was treated with more care, with Bath stone ashlar facings, a moulding around the aperture, and topped by an elegant parapet — all in the neo-classical style to match the elegance of nearby Bath. The portal of the 200m long Middle Hill tunnel further west is arguably an even better classical design but at Twerton tunnel, west of Bath, Brunel reverted to his favoured castelated Gothic.

In Edinburgh, the classical elegance of the architecture of the New Town was matched by the particularly fine stone portal of the Scotland Street tunnel, opened in 1847 on what was then the main line to the north from Waverley station. Half a mile long it was short lived, as it was bypassed in 1868.

56   *Tunnels were not only expensive in financial terms but also in lives; Bramhope tunnel, Yorkshire, finished in 1849, was 2¼ miles long and 23 workers died building it. They are commemorated in the churchyard at nearby Otley in a monumental replica of the north portal.*

Once a tunnel was completed, it was usual to fill in some of the working shafts but others would be left open for ventilation and for maintenance purposes. To protect anyone from falling down the shaft top would be carried up as a small tower, capped by a grill and sometimes fitted with an access door. They were usually built of plain brick and cylindrical but occasionally these turrets became an excuse for some architectural humour. Whilst the two very large brick towers over the 'great shafts' of the Kilsby tunnel were unusual, similar battlements on even the smallest of air shafts were not. Presumably the small expense incurred was worth paying to pacify the landowner, or for sheer whimsy, and all now have had a century or so to weather and blend into the scenery. Often associated with them are overgrown undulations in the ground pointing to where much of the excess spoil from the tunnel workings went.

The once most famous of all cut-and-cover tunnels are now taken for granted. These are the shallower tunnels of the London Underground, developed from the late nineteenth century and still being extended. The first of these was the section of the mixed-gauge Metropolitan Railway between Bishop's Road, Paddington and Farringdon Street, opened in 1863. The line was engineered by John Fowler (later of Forth Bridge fame) and for four miles ran through a densely populated part of West London. A deep cutting was initially dug, mainly in the middle of existing streets, but even so up to 1000 houses were demolished in the process. The cutting was then lined and roofed with a

57   *Finding uses for redundant tunnels is not always easy. The 2ft 6in gauge Manifold Light Railway in North Staffordshire was not a success and closed in 1935. The trackbed was given to the county council who, with great foresight, made it into a footpath and cycleway in 1937. A short section is used by cars, and this includes the Swainsley tunnel.*

mixture of brick and iron arching, and rubble and soil was then added to restore the ground surface. One of the most unusual legacies of this line, incidentally, was on the later extension west of Paddington where much of it ran in a cutting. In Leinster Gardens, the building of the line created a gap in a recently built terrace of houses. Two dummy facades, Nos. 23 and 25, were built to fill the gap, virtually on the edge of the cutting.

The later 'deep' tunnel lines, or 'tubes' were mainly built at the end of the nineteenth century and into the twentieth and, whilst still extraordinary feats of engineering, benefited greatly from the experiences of earlier tunnels and vastly improved tunnelling techniques. There are well over 200 miles of underground railways beneath the capital and the Northern line runs in a continuous tunnel between East Finchley and Morden that is well over 17 miles long. Opened in 1939 it was, until 1988, the longest railway tunnel in the world.

III: Buildings
9 General

Tens of thousands of buildings were built and used by the railways, ranging in size and grandeur from the humble platelayer's lineside hut to the Gothic extravagance of Scott's Midland Hotel at St. Pancras. Some — such as engine sheds and the signal boxes — were developed specifically for railway purposes and had no obvious historical precedents that could be followed. Nevertheless the railway companies in the nineteenth century also built thousands of 'ordinary' buildings — houses, warehouses, and workshops for example.

There are, understandably, very few buildings surviving that were associated with the early waggonways and plateways. Most of these early lines were built simply to connect pits to wharves or different industrial sites and had no need of any buildings other than those associated with the engineering of the line. Stables and stores may have been built to serve such a railway but these would have indistinguishable from other buildings of the same type in the same area.

The earliest surviving 'railway' building is probably the former weigh house on the Brampton Railway at Brampton Sands, built in 1799. By far the grandest plateway building was built by the Coalbrookdale Company by the banks of the Severn. The castellated brick warehouse and transhipment building of the 1830s still retains in its brick paved floor and sloping quay the channels in which the plateways ran; it is now part of the Ironbridge Gorge Museum Trust. By the time that warehouse was built, the steam railway had been established and the 'Railway Revolution' that resulted led to a massive explosion in the number of railway related buildings.

10 Stations

The railway station was and still is the most public of all railway buildings. The station was entirely a new invention of the railways; the concept of a special and specific place at which passengers could buy their tickets, wait for their transport, get on board and, at the end of their journey, subsequently dismount, was not one that existed for the passenger travelling by road or canal. Coach and wagon passengers had usually bought their tickets at, and waited in, a suitable hostelry. Canals were concerned almost exclusively with the transport of merchandise and the few passengers that were taken simply turned up at the wharf and were carried on a largely *ad hoc* basis. There were a few regular passenger services, and a small ticket office survives on the Bridgewater Canal at Worsley, but there was nothing as ambitious for the canal passenger as even the humblest country railway station.

Like the canals, none of the earliest railways had really considered passenger carrying as a priority. The Oystermouth Railway's pioneering service in south Wales, started in 1807, was very much the exception rather than the rule — and had ceased by 1826. The Stockton & Darlington Railway's passengers were initially transported in horse-drawn coaches and were treated in much the same way as stage coach passengers, buying their tickets and waiting at local inns; there were no stations as such, just pick-up points with no platforms or proper facilities. Thus the cottage by the level-crossing in St. John's Road, Stockton-on-Tees, was hardly a station at all in the modern sense of the word. There was no proper station on the line until North Road, Darlington, opened in 1833.

The first attempts at proper passenger accommodation were on the Liverpool & Manchester Railway. The company built purpose-built termini at either end of the line for the opening in 1830, though both were short-lived as passenger stations. The Manchester terminus on Liverpool Road was to prove untypical of the stations that were to follow. Architecturally it was very restrained, and on the Liverpool Road itself looks little more than two substantial town houses side by side, one of brick, the other faced in stucco. The brick building is, in fact, a substantial town house; it was built in 1809 and was bought by the railway company for the station agent. The stuccoed building built next to it was built by the railway, probably to the designs of Thomas Haigh of Liverpool.

At ground floor level there were separate booking offices for first and second class passengers and stairs led up to separate waiting rooms on the first floor — which was at the level of the tracks. A simple king-post timber roof provided shelter to the main platform. Added alongside the main station were goods and parcels offices and, at street level, some shops the company let out until they needed the room; above, the first-floors

58   *Despite being carefully restored to something like its original 1836 condition, the former Liverpool & Manchester Railway station at Edge Hill, Liverpool, is rather lost amongst the later changes made to the line. The building on the left is probably the oldest station building still used for its original purpose.*

are facades in front of the former carriage shed. All in all, the Liverpool Road station was built to fit in with the streetscape, not, as most later urban stations would do, deliberately to stand out from it.

In 1844 Liverpool Road station was superseded by a new station closer to the city centre at Hunts Bank, soon renamed Manchester Victoria. Fortunately, it was converted to purely goods use and remained remarkable unaltered until being closed in 1975. Subsequently it has been restored to as near to its original state as possible and is the oldest passenger station in the world.

At the other end of the Liverpool & Manchester Railway the original terminus in Crown Street was also a modest in comparison to what was to follow. It had a plain late-Georgian two-storey station house containing offices on the first floor and a combined ticket office and waiting room on the ground floor; the platform was covered and there was an additional canopy over the tracks. The station was short lived; it was too far away from the middle of Liverpool and as early as 1836 the line was extended to a new terminus in Lime Street. Crown Street was closed to passengers and became a repair and goods depot; another new station was built nearby at Edge Hill — possibly designed by Haigh as well. There are no traces left of the Crown Street station today, but Edge Hill was carefully restored by British Rail in the late 1970s when later additions were removed and

59   Whilst London Euston could boast the fine portico and magnificent Great Hall, its platform area was not as impressive as most of its main rivals. The simple iron platforms were, nevertheless, the oldest in the country and had been designed by Robert Stephenson. Ex-LMS Jubilee 45666 Cornwallis *prepares to depart in December 1962, shortly before the old station was demolished.*

the original buildings repaired. The simple and vaguely classical buildings on each platform have deep rusticated ashlared stonework; that on the north platform is still in use as a ticket office and can thus claim to be the oldest station building still being used for its original purpose. The brick structures next to it are the remains of the winding engine house built in the 1840s to work the Lime Street incline, which was only converted to locomotive haulage in about 1870.

The Edge Hill station buildings differed from the earlier ones on the line by not pretending to be something else. From then on most station buildings would announce themselves to the travelling public by their architecture and style. This was especially so in the larger towns, and from the late-1830s to the 1870s, railway companies vied with each other to provide the most magnificent buildings, testing engineering skills to the limit in the process.

Nowhere was this more so than in London, and the first dramatic example was the Euston terminus of the London & Birmingham, opened in 1837, the capital's first main line station. The city fathers were determined to keep the railway outside the centre of London, which is why most of the earlier termini — Euston, Paddington, London Bridge, and King's Cross — are virtually in the suburbs. At Euston there was originally just a glazed multi-pitched iron train shed designed by Robert Stephenson on the platforms.

Then, in 1840, the famous portico, or propylaeum, was built in stone from Yorkshire on Euston Square to the designs of Philip Hardwick. This extravagant but functionally useless Doric masterpiece announced the arrival of the railway in the capital, and was, literally, the gateway to the Midlands and the North. It was, however, soon hemmed in by other buildings and the grand setting was rather disfigured. At the other end of the line, in Curzon Street, Birmingham, Hardwick built a similar, but slightly smaller, portico.

A little later, in 1849, Hardwick's son, Philip C. Hardwick, built the splendid Great Hall at Euston, between the gateway and station shed. This huge double-storied space with its 61 feet (18.6m) wide coffered ceiling was a much rarer element in the great stations, one nearly contemporary example being that at the Low Level station in Wolverhampton finished in 1855. The Wolverhampton station, now disused, survives virtually intact though awaiting redevelopment.

All of the Euston buildings, apart from the later pavilions flanking the portico, were controversially demolished in the early 1960s to make way for the present wind-swept, uncompromising and characterless complex of today. Fortunately, Curzon Street station was quickly by-passed and was demoted to a goods depot early on; its portico, happily, still stands. These detached entrances did not catch on, though the Shrewsbury & Birmingham Railway did build something similar in Queen Street, Wolverhampton, at the approach to their original High Level station of 1848. Used for many years as railway offices, and then for too many years derelict, this building has recently been restored and, ironically, is part of a new bus-station.

Railway stations had a specific function and within a few years of the opening of the Liverpool & Manchester Railway general characteristics evolved. One particularly British development was the 'high' platform. Early carriages had running boards or steps up to the doors so early platforms were quite low. The small station at Heighington in County Durham, on the Stockton & Darlington Railway, is thought to date from the 1830s and retains a low cobbled platform. By the 1860s higher platforms were being built that allowed easier access for passengers, even on the humblest of railways. The typical sloped ends of these higher platforms were the result of Board of Trade regulations. On the Continent and in North America, the combination of low platforms and carriage steps has continued, with only a few exceptions.

The relatively low capacity of traffic in these early days meant that there was not a great deal of pressure on platform space at the stations and train movements were few. Although both Manchester Liverpool Road and Liverpool Crown Street stations had just one platform, it soon became more common for termini to have two — one for departures and one for arrivals. Space between the main running lines to these platforms was taken up by carriage sidings. On intermediate stations, especially on double lines, it made sense to have two platforms, one for each direction. This was usually the case on single lines as well, the stations being used as loops where trains could cross. Usually the platforms were opposite each other, with the main station buildings on one side (usually nearest to the centre of the town or village) and secondary ones on the other. Sometimes the platforms would be staggered on either side of a bridge or a level crossing.

However, at some stations some companies, notably the Great Western, only had platforms on one side of the station. Brunel was largely responsible for this. At Reading,

60   Simple, and elegant, Canterbury West, Kent, is one of the finer small stations of the South
Eastern Railway and opened in 1849. The architect was probably Samuel Beazley, who
designed the more elaborate SER station at Gravesend, Kent. This view was taken in 1978.

for example, he had separate platforms on the town side of the station for trains running
in different directions, the idea being that passengers would not have to cross the line.
Each platform had its own accommodation and its own staff and was, in effect, almost a
completely separate station. This layout meant that trains had to cross over the tracks to
the platforms, leading to unnecessary wear and tear on points and signals and being
potentially dangerous. At the last major station to be laid out in this way, the Low Level
station at Wolverhampton ready by 1854, the dangers were compounded by the fact that
the main line entered a tunnel just a few yards from the station. Despite all these
problems, several major stations — such as Cambridge, Chester and Derby, started off
with a single platform. This does account for some of the very long frontages of such
stations of the 1840s and the opportunity this offered in the case of these three for their
architect, Francis Thompson.

By the second half of the nineteenth century it was far more common to have more
platforms. At the main termini, the carriage sidings between the original platforms were
gradually colonised by new platforms as the number of train movements increased and the
small carriage turntables became obsolete as carriage size grew. At major intermediate
stations, additional platforms were added alongside the old ones, or bay platforms were
created. Even relatively small stations were often given bay platforms, especially if they
dealt with a branch line. Other bay platforms were used for goods traffic.

61   *Sir William Tite was one of the most respected station architects of his day and produced many different types of designs. This is the facade of his station at Winchester, Hampshire, built in 1839 for the London & South Western Railway (Ken Hoverd/Archive 1994).*

The growth in the number of platforms also meant that passengers had to be provided with a means of getting over the tracks to them. At the terminus this was not a problem, but at through stations, underpasses or, more commonly, footbridges, had to be provided. Pedestrian level crossings were frowned upon by the Board of Trade, though many stations retained them. A large number of elegant cast or wrought-iron footbridges survive from the 1880s onwards. Unfortunately, many of the expensive subways, with their walls of glazed white brick and ingenious lighting arrangements, have become easy targets for vandals and graffiti.

A late development in Britain, at the end of the nineteenth century, was the island platform; in this arrangement the main running lines pass on either side of a broad, single platform. It cut down on the need for passengers to cross the tracks, and on the numbers of staff and facilities required at the station. Obviously there had to be access to the platform in the first place. This was often achieved by placing the main entrance to the station on the side of a road bridge across the railway and having steps down from it to the platform. It proved very useful for suburban stations, such as those on the Great Western main line in south Birmingham. Some island platforms were broad enough to accommodate bay platforms at one or both ends. Larger stations could have a combination

62   *Ridgmont is one of four pretty stations built in the* cottage ornée *style by the Bedford Railway in 1846, each to a slightly different design. Despite being a listed building, it is empty and had been allowed to fall into a shocking state of repair by 1998.*

of island, single and bay platforms — typical examples being Edinburgh Waverley, Crewe, and Shrewsbury — much of the latter being built on a bridge over the River Severn.

Few of the original stations in the major towns have survived, largely because of the initial underestimating of potential passenger traffic and later sharing arrangements as more and more companies built more and more railways. A few stations were only temporary, such as the first ones at London Paddington and Wolverhampton. The loss of Euston station in the 1960s was followed by the partial loss of a second and historically important major station — York. The city's first station was built inside the city walls, and two arches were cut through the city walls, the first in 1839 being designed by George T. Andrews. Andrews also designed the station buildings erected in 1840 and jointly owned by George Hudson's York & North Midlands and Great North of England railways, and the latter's engineer, George Stephenson, probably helped to design the track layout of the terminus. The platforms and tracks were covered initially by a double-span iron roof but as the traffic grew additional platforms and canopies were provided along with more station buildings and a hotel, also by Andrews.

Its cramped site, and the fact that through trains called at it despite the fact it was a terminus, made it difficult to work and by the 1860s plans were made to replace it; these did not come to fruition until 1877. It was demoted to goods use but was still virtually intact at the start of the 1960s, despite some ugly brick additions. In 1965-6 British

63   *Cemmaes Road station, Powys, is typical of many small country stations throughout Britain that survived closure to be converted into housing despite still being on a 'live' railway line — in this case the former Cambrian Railways main route to the Welsh coast. Both the attractive stone station and the matching station master's house are lived in.*

Railways demolished the historic platform canopies and the platforms to make room for a new regional headquarters that has since been demolished in turn. Most of the original station buildings have survived, but the site is currently being redeveloped again.

For the most part the earliest surviving stations are those in the small to medium sized towns and in rural areas. Being far more numerous they are also far more typical of the age than the prodigy stations of the capital and the major urban centres. Whilst the facilities offered by the different grades of stations were generally similar from company to company, the architectural styles chosen for the buildings and structures in which these were presented varied enormously. The architecture of stations can, in a very real way, tell a great deal of the aspirations of the companies that built them and their construction also reflects the development of contemporary engineering techniques — and confidence.

Contemporary Victorian critics, like the eccentric John Ruskin, did not consider railway architecture to be true architecture at all. Architecture was, he declared in his influential *Seven Lamps of Architecture,* different from mere building and there was a definite sublime art that 'separates architecture from a wasp's nest, a rat hole, or a railway station'. Ruskin did not like railways, and all that they stood for. A station, for him, was 'the very temple of discomfort' but he did have a valid point when asking if a passenger on the London & South Western would be willing to pay higher fares 'because the columns of the terminus [Waterloo] are covered with patterns from Nineveh'.

117

64   *Crewe is one of the most important junctions on the whole railway system yet its station, despite this, has never been an architectural masterpiece. Several half-hearted attempts to modernise it have never eliminated its rather ramshackled charm. This is a view of the station in 1987.*

The steam railway era began at a time when the architectural certainties were breaking down. The long era of classical and neo-classical styles, effectively beginning, after some false and isolated starts, with the Palladian revival in the early eighteenth century, was ending and fragmenting. The work of Robert Adam, James Wyatt, and John Soane, to name just three of the more influential architects of the later eighteenth century, had begun to blur the architectural rules and in the stylistic vacuum of the early nineteenth century there was also a growing use of deliberately Picturesque versions of older non-classical styles. Revivals included everything from serious medieval Gothic to playful cottage Tudor and there was thus a vast array of possible styles for the railway companies to use.

There was usually a difference in the styles chosen for urban and rural stations. This was partly because of the scale of the buildings required, partly because of their relative importance to the railway companies, and partly because of the demands, directly or indirectly, of local landowners. In the countryside, stations, particularly up until the 1850s, had to be seen to be attractive elements of the landscape and to give the impression that they had always been part of it. At the same time they also had to reflect the new world of the railways. This dual function was probably the reason why the buildings at most country stations were very similar to the lodges of the large country houses. By the nineteenth century the gate lodge was a familiar type of building and, whilst not usually large, it did allow for a degree of architectural pretension lacking in a normal cottage. The stations were, in effect, the lodges to the great railway network and they too could be decorated accordingly. Indeed, the series of neat designs by Francis Thompson on the North Midland Railway were used as the basis for villas in John C. Loudon's *Encyclopaedia of Cottage, Farm and Villa Architecture* of 1842.

On very rare occasions existing buildings could be adapted for station use, though there are often academic disputes as to the truth of such traditions. One reasonably certain example survives at Mitcham, Surrey, where the entranceway to the Wimbledon & Croydon's station of 1855 was through what seems to be a three-bay three-storey late-Georgian house. At the other extreme, the first 'building' on the Shrewsbury & Hereford Railway's Moreton-on-Lugg station, opened in 1852, was the hollowed-out stump of an oak tree called Adam — one of a pair with the 'more comely' Eve in the nearby field; it had been superseded by proper buildings within a few years.

One of the oldest surviving country stations is that at Felling, built in 1839 on the Brandling Junction Railway connecting South Shields and Gateshead — now part of the Tyne & Wear Metro. Constructed of local sandstone, it has a double-pile body with a projecting wing containing a large three-light Tudor window which lit the combined ticket office and waiting room. Amazingly, despite being closed to passengers in 1896 and being left derelict until the 1970s, it has survived. A major repair in 1978 radically rebuilt the upper part and roof.

Most companies built reasonably pleasant rural stations, but some stand out amongst the rest. The North Staffordshire Railway built in a consistent Jacobean house-style typified by tall curving gables; unlike most companies they used this for both their town and village stations. Amongst the best surviving examples of each are Sandon, a large station for a small village built in 1849 to pacify the owner of Sandon Hall, the Earl of Harrowby, and the main station in Stoke on Trent. That building, and the nearby North Stafford Hotel, were designed by H.A.Hunt, who probably designed some of the other stations as well.

Crossing the north of England, the Newcastle & Carlisle Railway opened in 1838 and its stations have been recognised as one of the most attractive, and least altered, series still in use. They are all built to a similar neo-Tudor theme in local stone but each is subtly different from the other; several boast a gabled oriel. The architect responsible was probably Benjamin Green, who later designed the slightly larger but not dissimilar stations on the Newcastle & Berwick Railway opened in 1847.

In the south-east of England there is a particularly attractive set of cottage ornéee stations built in 1846 by the Bedford Railway on the line from that town to Bletchley — which was quickly taken over by the London & North Western Railway. Their mock timber-framing and elaborate details are straight out of one of the many pattern books for lodges and ornamental cottages published in the 1830s and 40s. Nearby the Duke of Bedford's Woburn estate, and the local villages, were similarly adorned with picturesque buildings for his workers though none quite like these stations.

Not all companies had the same approach to the size or style of their rural stations, either for economic or other reasons. There is a strong contrast, for example, in the intermediate country stations of the almost contemporary Shrewsbury & Chester and Shrewsbury & Birmingham Railways, built in the late 1840s and sharing a fine Tudor-

Gothic joint station in Shrewsbury designed by Thomas Penson. Penson also designed the stations on the Shrewsbury & Chester, giving each its individual style — Rednal was a little like a Tudor yeoman's house, Rossett was a cottage ornée, and Gobowen a rather fine stuccoed Italianate villa to list just three. In contrast, on the Shrewsbury & Birmingham, the stations were all designed, probably by the line's engineer William Baker, to a definite and rather dull brick house style with plain Italianate decoration; only at the terminus in Wolverhampton — a victim of 1960s' rebuilding — was any great architectural effort made.

Of the larger companies, the Great Western Railway was originally a little mean with its country stations, many being quite small and built to a standard Brunel design or variants of it. The buildings could be built in brick, stone or timber and usually featured deep integral canopies. Architecturally they were either vaguely Italianate or neo-Tudor, depending on the location. At Yatton, opened in 1841 on the Bristol & Exeter line, there are two Brunel buildings — one a standard Tudor design, the other an Italianate design modified with Tudor detailing. The best surviving example of a small standard Brunel station is that at Culham, Oxfordshire, opened in 1844.

The facilities of country stations to a great degree depended on their size and importance and on any influence that a local landowner may have had. All stations were staffed and the station master usually lived in the station house. In England and Wales this was almost always of two storeys, with the station master and his family living on the first floor above the ticket office and waiting room. Some companies built separate station master's houses instead, and single storey station offices. A large number of Scottish stations were of single storey, with the stationmasters house built next to the booking office; this was not to save money but more in keeping with the traditional village buildings. There were exceptions, of course, such as the sole surviving original station on the Aberdeen Railway at Stonehaven, built in 1850, which has station master's accommodation on the first floor.

Basic station facilities included a shelter, usually a short canopy attached to the main building over the platform door of the booking office, and public toilets. Larger village stations may have a more elaborate canopy and could be given more than one waiting room. Usually, these facilities were only on the platform next to the station building and only later were shelters added on the opposite platform. By the time these waiting rooms were added, many of the small independent companies had become part of much larger concerns and there is much greater uniformity, and some dullness, in their architecture. They were seldom designed to fit in with the original buildings and, because of the cheapness of transporting materials that the railways had themselves brought about, they were often built of brick or prefabricated mass-produced timber 'kits'. Most country stations also dealt with goods and parcels traffic, usually having a short bay platform.

Later stations in the countryside, built from the 1860s onwards, tended to decline in architectural quality. The railway by this time was an accepted part of life and was no longer held in awe or trepidation and most of the later lines tended also to be ones built in less potentially profitable areas.

After the opening of the Liverpool & Manchester Railway the railways stations in towns were not only larger than their rural counterparts but had a different status in the urban architectural hierarchy. They were no longer subservient lodges but symbols of the

65   *Frome, Somerset, is the only all-wooden 'Brunel barn' still in existence, even though it was actually designed by one of his assistants, J R Hannaford; it opened in 1850 on the Wilts., Somerset & Weymouth Railway. A local train calls at the station in April 1988.*

wealth, innovation and economic success of the new railways. Their architecture was designed to inspire confidence and custom, and their operating requirements led to the development of new and exciting structural techniques.

Initially, the style chosen by most companies for town stations was that last and much debased neo-classicism prevalent in urban domestic architecture — though there are also many examples of much more intelligent and more aesthetically pleasing approach. Amongst the finest true neo-classical station buildings are those at Huddersfield, designed by James Pritchett, boasting a Corinthian portico and opened in 1847, and at Monkwearmouth, County Durham, by John Dobson with its bold Greek Revival Ionic portico opened a year later. Both of those were built in ashlared stone suitable to the task, but at the Wolverhampton Low Level station built for the Oxford, Worcester & Wolverhampton Railway in 1855, the architect managed to produce a very finely proportioned facade using blue engineering brick and stone details. Facing this, the rival High Level station built a long Roman colonnade as part of the pedestrian link between the two stations, which survived the rebuilding of the station in the 1960s. These buildings represent the last gasp of proper classicism in railway architecture, and were built at a time when the popularity of diluted Italianate style and a deliberate vernacular historicism reached new heights.

66   *Most critics regard Lewis Cubitt's functional but elegant King's Cross station as one of the finest pieces of pure railway architecture and have done since it opened in 1852 as the London terminus of the Great Northern Railway. The huge glazed arched windows pierce a simple brick screen and reflect the twin trainsheds behind; there is little or no unnecessary ornament.*

One aspect of the larger stations was the shelter provided for the passengers, pioneered on the Liverpool & Manchester Railway. Euston was the first major station to have such an all-over roof, but one made up of several low interconnected roofs supported on cast iron or wooden piers. This system had the advantage of being relatively cheap and easy to extend or adapt, and was widely copied throughout the country. However, the amount of pillars interfered with the movement of passengers, goods and luggage, and if just one of them was damaged in some way, the whole roof structure could become unsafe. The ideal solution was to create wider spanned overall roofs, and gradually these became not just aids to better station management, but status symbols for the railway companies.

When the Great Western Railway opened throughout in 1841 there was only a temporary terminus in London. At the other end of the line was Brunel's Bristol Temple Meads terminus, ready the previous year. For the main station building, Brunel designed a Tudor-Gothic style — dismissed as 'engineer's Gothic' by Pugin — in honey coloured stone. Behind it the arrival and departure platforms and the sidings between were covered by an overall roof or train shed. This was a magnificent and very wide timber structure supported by mock-hammerbeams. Subsequently, in 1878, a new joint station was built by the Great Western and the Midland railways and the original was demoted to lesser

67 *A detail of the wonderfully fluid ironwork of the trainshed at London Paddington; although Brunel's influence was all pervading, the architectural details were by Matthew Digby Wyatt.*

usage. By the 1970s it had no tracks at all and was a rather run-down car park, but it was, happily, restored in the early 1980s. Brunel also used timber for the canopies of most of his intermediate stations, and the larger ones were also given overall roofs, much simpler timber-framed structures faced with weather boarding and often nicknamed the 'Brunel Barns'. Of these only that at Frome survives, and this was designed not by Brunel but by his assistant, J R Hannaford, for the Wilts, Somerset & Weymouth Railway in 1850. Curiously, although the design was seldom used elsewhere in England or Wales, two small terminus stations in the far north of Scotland — Wick and Thurso on the Sutherland & Caithness Railway opened in 1874 — were given similar overall roofs.

The loss of the original Euston station means that the earliest main line terminus in London is now nearby King's Cross, finished in 1852. In many ways this was actually a much better architectural design and one of the few major stations that even Ruskin may have liked. His only words of comfort for railways in the *Seven Lamps* were that 'Railroad

68   Only inside St. Pancras can the sheer size of Barlow's single span train shed be really
        appreciated. The resulting clear span available for railway operations was, and is, unrivalled.
        It is difficult to realise that there is another whole floor of store rooms beneath track level. This
        is the view looking towards the buffer stops in 1987.

architecture has, or would have, a dignity of its own if it were only left to its work.' King's
Cross station is one in which this was more or less the case; it was built to a very simple
design and its principal architect, Lewis Cubitt, was clearly proud of 'its fitness for its
purpose, and its characteristic expression of that purpose'. Whilst larger than Euston, it
cost half the amount to build.

The two great curved arched roofs of King's Cross station, both 32m wide and 244m
long, were made up of laminated wooden girders and were expressed in the unadorned
stock-brick facade as deeply recessed arches. Even the one ornament on the facade, the
clock tower between the arches (a repeat of the clock at his earlier London Bridge station),
was a functional feature — time, and specifically uniform railway time, being of vital
importance to the new era. The main station buildings were not built at the end of the
platforms, but along one side — the other being used for the hackney cabs. At track level
there was one departure and one arrival platform, with 14 lines for carriages in between;
gradually these were colonised by more platforms. The laminated arches were short lived;
the east shed arches were replaced with wrought-iron girders in 1870 and the west side
ones in 1887. Many of the later accretions in front of the station were swept away when
the building was restored a few years ago — but unfortunately replaced by modern ones.

69   *Opulent and ostentatious, the Midland Railway's St. Pancras was a marked contrast to King's*
      Cross next door — but the comparison is a little unfair. Sir George Gilbert Scott's hugely over-
      the-top Gothic romp on the Euston Road is, after all, mainly an hotel rather than a station.
      Barlow's trainshed behind was an engineering triumph when finished in 1868, five years
      before the hotel.

King's Cross was not the first station to boast a fine arched-roofed trainshed. In 1849-51 Liverpool Lime Street had been rebuilt and given a single span roof based on 'crescent' or 'quarter moon' trussed girders. It was designed by Richard Turner, Joseph Locke, and William Fairbairn. Turner was the main contractor, and was also involved in the famous Palm House at Kew Gardens, and the ironwork was made in his Dublin works. When complete, the roof was 46.6m wide, 112.8m long overall, and a little under 18.3m high; it was the largest trainshed in the world when it opened and the first to be constructed entirely of iron.

Further north, the underrated architect John Dobson had designed the train shed for Newcastle Central, opened in 1850. To do so he invented bevelled rollers that could make the wrought iron girders into the correct shapes in the foundry, and the resultant three parallel curving 55 foot span roofs were tremendously influential. The first to copy the basic concept was the Great Western Railway. They had originally intended to share the Euston terminus of the London & Birmingham, but the companies not only disagreed on minor things, but also adopted different gauges, making sharing difficult. The scheme was dropped and the Great Western built their own temporary terminus at Paddington.

70   *There was a brief vogue for prestigious trainsheds influenced by St. Pancras and that at Manchester Central shows its origins quite clearly. Opened in 1880 by the Cheshire Lines Committee, of which the Midland Railway was one of three partners, it never had the promised grand façade and made do with a selection of 'temporary' buildings until it closed in 1969. In the early 1980s work was underway to convert it into the GMex exhibition centre — an innovative use for an important building.*

This was completely rebuilt between 1850 and 1854 by Brunel and the architect Matthew Digby Wyatt, who added some vaguely Moorish touches particularly in the cast-iron work. The contractors were Fox, Henderson & Co. Paddington Station was more cathedral-like than others because its three original great 213.4m long 'naves' of wrought-iron ribs supported on cast-iron columns were linked by two 'transepts'. The central span was over 30.5m wide and 15m high whilst the flanking ones, oddly, were slightly different in width — 20.7m and 21.2m. The 'transepts' were built to allow room for the 'traversers' which were to be used to move carriages bodily sideways from one track to another instead of the more cumbersome miniature turntables then used on most other stations; they were never installed. One other original innovation used at Paddington was Paxton's 'ridge-and-furrow' glazing that had recently been made famous by the Crystal Palace of 1851. Although this has now been replaced, the large carriage sidings between the four original platforms infilled with other platforms, the cast-iron columns replaced in steel, and a fourth span added in 1915, Paddington is one of the finer stations in the world of its date.

In the same year that Paddington was finished, the rebuilt Birmingham New Street station was open and its main arched span was 64.6m wide, beating that of Lime Street.

71 *York's curving trainshed is undoubtedly one of the most dramatic, if neither the widest or tallest, in Britain. Designed by Thomas Prosser for the North Eastern Railway it was finished in 1877. Note how only every third rib springs from a supporting Corinthian cast-iron pillar. This 1987 view shows an Inter-City 125 about to leave.*

Known originally as the Central Station, the engineers in charge were William Baker and E. A. Cowper; the roof was again built by the Fox, Henderson & Co. The station was altered later in the century and damaged by bombing in the Second World War before, like Euston, being redeveloped in the 1960s. The result is a characterless subterranean station that has to be one of the least attractive of the major stations in Europe.

The great decades for ambitious trainsheds were the 1860s and 1870s. In 1867 the main arched roof of the rebuilt Liverpool Lime Street station equalled that of New Street, and in the following year the Midland Railway's delayed access to London was finally opened. Their terminus, St. Pancras was, literally, over the road from King's Cross. The trainshed was designed by William Barlow and has the most magnificent span of all, 74m wide and 33.5m at the apex of its slightly pointed arch. The platforms are well above the ground level and there was room for a huge labyrinth of beer and store cellars underneath reached from the adjacent streets. At track level there was an overall iron deck that also served as a collar tie for the great wrought-iron arches supporting the roof.

St Pancras is probably more famous for its Midland Hotel than its train shed, the hotel being built to the Gothic Revival designs of George Gilbert Scott. Opened in 1876 it was a commercial failure and closed in 1935 since when finding a suitable use for this extraordinary building has been, and apparently still is, difficult. The contrast between the

72   *Many stations have surprising little hidden architectural gems. This is the beautifully tiled iron-framed waiting room in Worcester Shrub Hill. The iron work was local, from the Vulcan Works in the city, and the tiles were by Maw's & Co. of Shropshire. (Ken Hoverd/Archive, 1994).*

73   *Although most stations have the same functions, a few have additional ones that are not necessarily obvious. The many large doorway's piercing the wall of Sir William Tite's Windsor & Eton Riverside station of 1849 were built to allow easy access for the cavalry. The station was built for the London & South Western Railway, and, like the rival GWR station, had a separate Royal waiting room for Queen Victoria. (Ken Hoverd/Archive, 1993).*

hotel, which hides the great train shed beyond, and the King's Cross station is immense, but it should be remembered that it was primarily a hotel and not a station — although its ground floor was and is used for station purposes. It is gloriously over the top; according to the critic Kenneth Clark in his *Gothic Revival* it 'seems to combine the west end of a German cathedral with several Flemish town halls' and even its architect, in his *Recollections* thought it 'possibly too good for its purpose'.

Similar, but slightly smaller, single span train sheds to that at St. Pancras were built at Manchester Central (recently restored and converted to an exhibition centre), Glasgow St. Enoch, sadly demolished, and Glasgow Central, happily renovated. Other fine major stations of the period include the rebuilt London Bridge and Liverpool Street stations in London, and two wonderfully curving train sheds — the extensions to Bristol Temple Meads and the new York station of 1877 with its dramatically curving trainshed designed by Thomas Prosser. From the end of the nineteenth century the great and expensive trainsheds went out of fashion — partly because the ones that did exist would last for years and partly because they were seen as an unnecessary and extravagant expense. By the time

74   *The bold blood-red decoration of Chalk Farm tube station near Camden is typical of the many stations designed, in a very short time, by Leslie Green in the 1900s before his early death. His work began to give the whole disparate underground system a unity it had previously lacked.*

that most ambitious of railway companies, the Great Central Railway, arrived in London in 1899 their Marylebone terminus was a very subdued affair.

By and large the stations built by the 1870s proved to be durable and well designed and have seldom needed to be replaced on operational grounds. There have obviously been some exceptions, where stations have been merged in towns or been rebuilt after damage — particularly after the bombing of the Second World War. Nevertheless, wholesale rebuilding of stations — such as Birmingham Snow Hill in 1912 and Leamington Spa in 1938 — was unusual.

The need for new stations at the start of the twentieth century was not great, except for the growing network of underground lines being built, especially in London and its environs, and in Glasgow. In London the underground system had been developed initially in the same way as the over ground railways, with numbers of competing small and independent companies promoting and building lines. Each had their own house style and there was no overall uniformity. Radical changes, and fresh capital and impetus, began in 1900 with the arrival of the controversial American financier Charles Tyson Yerkes. He quickly took control of several lines built or building and formed the Underground Electric Railways Company largely with American backing. He hired the young architect Leslie Green in 1903 to build stations to a new company house style; in less than five years

75   *Green's work was followed by that of Charles Holden in between the world wars and although St. John's Wood station was built in 1939, to the designs of S. A. Heaps, it continued the new house style. An office block has recently been added alongside and above the station.*

Green designed over 40 stations but died aged just 33. His style made considerable use of glazed brick — a dark blood-red for surface buildings and white, with polychrome decoration and signage, for the tunnel and subway linings. The surface buildings made clever use of often restricted sites and bold use of moulded brick and arched windows and openings. They were also built strong enough to allow later revenue earning offices or apartments to be built on top of them.

After the First World War Green's successor was Charles Holden who replaced the more florid Edwardian style with a pioneering functional modernism first seen on the 1926 extension to Morden. Fine examples of his work include those on the 1932 northern extension of the Piccadily line at Arnos Grove, Oakwood, and Southgate. When the London Passenger Transport Board was set up by an Act of 1933 to take over the capital's underground and bus routes, Holden became their architect.

Above ground the competition from road transport after the First World War led to the creation of large numbers of new railway stations. These were similar to many stations built for the Light Railways after 1896. Most were very basic and generally unstaffed. They consisted of one or two platforms, usually wooden, with small shelters, also usually of timber. The Great Western Railway also used prefabricated buildings sheathed in corrugated iron, some of which had quite graceful roofs that led to them being called the 'Pagodas'.

76   *Not all stations were large. This tiny brick building, probably built in the 1880s, comprised all the station facilities at Pontfadog, Clwyd, and was on the 2ft 4¼in gauge Glyn Valley Tramway linking quarries at the west end of the valley with the main line at Chirk.*

Huge numbers of stations were closed in the 1950s and 60s and left to their fate. Some found new uses as houses, especially in the countryside, making ideal detached family homes — even if they are still on a 'live' line. A slightly different use was given to the Italianate station at Alton Towers, Staffordshire, on the picturesque Churnet Valley line of the North Staffordshire Railway opened in 1849. The line closed in 1965 but the station was given by the County Council to the Landmark Trust who have looked after it ever since as one of their famous historic holiday homes. Other country stations, though stripped of some of their buildings, have, like Tintern, Gwent, been adapted as picnic areas. A surprisingly large number are still in use, and perhaps better cared for than ever before, on the many preserved steam railways created in Britain since the 1960s.

In towns, some stations were converted to offices or industrial purposes. Generally, however, the land values in towns and the difficulties in converting large train sheds and platforms, have led eventually to demolition and redevelopment, often preceded by a long period of dereliction and vandalism — and in many cases, use for car parking. This was the fate of Birmingham Snow Hill, though the subsequent redevelopment included a new suburban station under the modern offices on a reinstated rail link. Several stations have been rescued from car park status and found innovative new uses; these include Manchester Central, now the Gmex Centre, and Bath Green Park, part of a supermarket.

These, it has to be said, are the exceptions. Even in the countryside, stations were often

77   *In the 1920s and 30s, in a bid to win back passengers from the growing bus networks, railway companies opened many basic stations, known as 'halts'. New Hadley Halt in Shropshire was typical, seen here in 1983, with its wooden platforms and, originally, shelters. Opened in the 1930s it survived longer than most, mainly because of the delays in building the new Telford Central station not far away.*

simply allowed to rot — and this is no longer confined to those buildings on abandoned lines. Further reduction in staffing from the 1970s has led to once quite important stations having their staff withdrawn from them and their buildings lying empty and subject to vandalism. This rich architectural heritage surely deserves better.

78   *A typical combined lamp standard and station sign, of which there were once tens of thousands. Colyford, Devon, was on the short Seaton branch of the London & South Western Railway which closed in 1966. In 1970 the line was reopened as the Seaton & Colyford Tramway, a 2ft 9in electric tramway.*

79   *A detail of a dated GWR cast-iron footbridge. Several of this standard pattern of footbridge can be found on the former GWR system, and those of other companies survive throughout the British rail network.*

11 Goods depots, sheds and warehouses

Railways evolved to carry goods, or, more specifically, minerals. Even though the passenger traffic took on a significance that no one had predicted after the opening of the Liverpool & Manchester Railway, goods traffic remained a vital part of the railway economy and many lines relied very heavily on it. Surviving buildings associated with this traffic predate the arrival of the steam locomotive.

In the nineteenth century even the smallest country station had a goods depot, usually served by a separate siding often ending in a bay on the main platform. Alternatively, the shed might be in a separate goods yard nearby and this probably had a weigh-bridge and weigh-bridge office. The goods shed had a simple function — the transfer and temporary storage of goods from road to rail or vice versa. This meant that there had to be a platform on which the goods could be unloaded from either the train or a horse-and-cart — and later, lorry. The goods could be transferred by hand or by a variety of trucks and barrows issued by the railway company.

Two basic types of shed evolved for smaller stations. In one the siding ran straight into the shed through an opening in the gable wall and in the other, it ran alongside the shed under a protective canopy. As with most ancillary railway buildings, these were built in whatever materials came to hand and seldom aspired to architectural pretensions. The surviving Great Western Railway shed outside Stroud station in Gloucestershire is one of the more attractive buildings of its type and has a four-centred Tudor-arched opening to the siding wide enough for the Broad Gauge trains for which it was originally built; it could have been, like the adjacent station, designed by Brunel.

Most stations had a crane to load and unload goods waggons as well. An important commodity carried by the railways was livestock, so most country stations had sidings that could be used for loading and unloading cattle and sheep. These usually had no associated buildings other than platforms and barriers with, possibly, some facilities to feed and water the animals.

In the main towns the railways usually built separate goods depots so as not to interfere with the normal passenger traffic at the ordinary stations. Their basic purpose was the same, but the capacities that could be dealt with were much larger. The one built by the Great Western Railway at Bristol Temple Meads grew until, in the 1950s, it covered 15 acres — all under cover. This was slightly larger in extent than the one built by the Midland Railway next to their London St. Pancras terminus. Inexplicably, the company

80   The odd slots in the sloping brick paving next to this building by the River Severn near Ironbridge were built to take the cast-iron L-section plateway rails of the Coalbrookdale's main line right to the waiting trows and barges on the river. Since this photograph of 1983, the former transhipment warehouse has been made into a museum; it was probably built in the 1830s.

delayed building on the land for some time and the new goods depot only opened in 1887. It was later known as the Somers Town goods station. Covering 14 acres in all it was built on two levels, a lower one at street level and an upper one 7.3m higher at the level of the tracks of the passenger station. Both were used by railway traffic. The upper deck was of iron, supposedly using no less than 20,000 tons of the material and claimed to be the largest in the world; it was supported by over 450 columns. The station has been demolished and the new British Library occupies the site.

Whilst most were purpose built, sometimes an old passenger station would be converted to goods use if it had been replaced. Typical examples of this include two of the earliest passenger stations, those at Liverpool Road Manchester on the Liverpool & Manchester and at Curzon Street, Birmingham on the London & Birmingham; both were demoted to goods traffic within years of opening. Other examples include the original stations at York and Selby, Yorkshire, the latter dating from 1834 and being replaced by a new station in 1891.

Larger good stations often included warehouses and perhaps the earliest to survive in more or less its original form is that at Liverpool Road, Manchester. Railway warehouses differed little from ordinary multi-storey warehouses other than having rail access. Good

81 Stroud goods shed still has the Great Western's name painted onto its side and was built for the Broad Gauge line between Swindon and Cheltenham opened in 1845. Brunel designed the nearby station and was probably also responsible for the goods shed with its Tudor rail entrance.

82 York had one of the larger goods depots, in Leeman Road between the station and the main engine sheds. It was remodelled in the 1890s and now houses a major extension of the excellent National Railway Museum.

83   *Small brick sheds like this one were once a common feature of goods depots and usually sited next to weighbridges. Weighbridges were either used for road or rail traffic. Hundreds of these buildings have been demolished since the early 1960s.*

84   *As part of British Railways Modernisation plan of the 1950s goods traffic was to be rationalised and large marshalling yards built at strategic points. Bescot, near Walsall, was one of these and is seen here in the early 1960s with the new electric wires up and diesels, rather than steam engines, in action. (British Rail, London Midland).*

85   *Wolverhampton Low Level station was once an important stop on the Great Western's main line from London to the Mersey. The fine station buildings survived closure of passenger services and, for a while, the station was used for parcels traffic. This view was taken in 1987, since when a scheme for a railway heritage centre was abandoned. The site is about to be redeveloped.*

examples survive in various parts of the country, ranging from ones for general storage to those designed for a specific one, such as the cloth warehouses of Lancashire and Yorkshire, the grain store at King's Cross, London, and the beer cellars under St. Pancras next door that accommodated the vast quantities of Burton beers transported to the capital by the Midland Railway.

Other types of goods facilities were those associated with wharves and docks. The earliest waggonways had run down to rivers and in the seventeenth century there is evidence that special loading wharves were built on the Tyne and the Severn by which waggons could be loaded directly onto waiting barges. In the north-east of England these were called *staithes* and became quite sophisticated steam-powered appliances.

More typical was the transhipment shed, which was little different than a standard goods depot other than the fact that the goods were being transferred between rail and water. A rather fine example of such a depot is at the bottom end of the Coalbrookdale at Dale End, where the plateway system ends in a mock-Gothic warehouse and there are still cuts in the sloping brick wharf that took the plateway tracks down to the water's edge. At the top end of the dale was a more remarkable, if short-lived, transfer system involving early containerisation; by the 1790s loads were taken off the small tub-boats at the end of the western arm of the Shropshire Canal by huge cranes and lowered down a shaft at the

86   *The military had several large bases with internal railway systems and several retained them until the 1980s. This is one of the largest, COD Donnington, Shropshire, and in 1984, a short train, hauled by one of the depot's small diesel shunters, has just emerged from one of the huge storage sheds.*

foot of which was a tunnel in which ran a plateway. The containers were simply loaded onto a waggon on the plateway and taken by rail for the rest of their journey. In some cases, rail-canal interchanges were built, sometimes with both a siding and a branch of the canal running in to either side of a loading platform inside a shed.

Other interchanges simply had railway siding running from the main line to the canal. Several of these existed long before the steam era, notably those at Froghall in Staffordshire and at Buxworth, Derbyshire established by the end of the eighteenth century. At Wolverhampton the Shrewsbury & Birmingham Railway built a large goods depot at Corn Hill close to the High Level station in 1849, probably designed by William Baker. In dispute with their erstwhile London & North Western Railway partners at the station, the S&C were eventually forced to join sides with the rival Great Western Railway in 1854 and moved to the Low Level station. Their old goods yard was transferred to the L&NWR but they seem not to have made much use of it; it still survives. As well as road access it was built next to the Birmingham Canal, as was the new depot built by the displaced S&C at the Victoria Basin further to the north. Smaller examples are fairly numerous and their remains are relatively easy to trace. At Rednal, sidings from the Shrewsbury & Chester Railway served a purpose built arm off the Shropshire Union's Llanymynech branch canal but this was not a success; the canal has recently been restored at this point and the old basin is now a nature reserve.

87   *In the First World War Richborough, Kent, was the site of a huge secret military port. Some of the sheds survive but little is left of the old port or the extensive rail network. This photograph was taken in 1978.*

88   *Many industrial railways, particularly those associated with quarrying, were built to a narrow gauge to save on costs. The Snailbeach District Railways (sic), built to a gauge of 2ft 3¾in, served the lead mining area of Shropshire and there are many surviving traces left. This long siding is at Snailbeach, and the building on the right is the former locomotive shed. That has been restored since this photograph was taken in 1981.*

Virtually all docks became linked to the rail network and usually rails were laid right onto the quayside. Sometimes this was by the railway companies but several of the major docks, such as London and Bristol, had their own rail systems. Some railway companies invested in their own docks, one of the earliest being the horse-drawn Carmarthenshire Railway which bought the docks at Llanelly and built a line to it in 1806 to export coal. In 1852 Grimsby docks in Lincolnshire were completely rebuilt with all the latest equipment by the Manchester, Sheffield & Lincoln Railway and they later, under their new name — the Great Central — built brand new docks at Immingham just down the coast just before the First World War.

During that war one of the largest, short-lived, and most secret of railway ports was built in the marshlands of the Stour estuary separating the Isle of Thanet from 'mainland' Kent. Richborough Port was developed as the major transhipment depot for war materials and troops sent to and from the Western Front in France. It was also the terminus of the first cross-channel rail ferry, used for military traffic. After the war the ferries and the docking equipment was reused for the first civilian cross-channel services from Harwich.

12 Locomotive sheds and works

The earliest 'engine sheds' were really the stables provided for the horses used on waggonways and plateways and these varied hugely in scale and design. As most followed local vernacular traditions it is very difficult to identify which of the surviving stable blocks reasonably near the routes of old railways were directly associated with them. Those most unfortunate animals — the pit ponies — had their stables deep underground and seldom saw the light of day.

The new 'iron horses', the steam locomotives of the 1820s and 30s, were very expensive to build and thus needed to be protected. An *Illustrated London News* article about Crewe in 1849 referred to the 'great engine-stable, into which the hot dusty locomotives are conducted after their journeys to be cleaned, examined, repaired, or if sound, to be greased and otherwise prepared for their departure.' Despite the apt parallels between servicing and sheltering horse and machine, the term 'locomotive stable' was scarcely ever used. However, engines are described as being 'stabled' at specific depots and tracks within depots are sometimes referred to as 'stalls'. 'Engine shed' became by far the commonest term, but 'running shed' was also used; by British Rail days the more pedantic 'Motive Power Depot' was in official use.

The term 'shed', certainly in use by the 1850s, may have been derogatory at first, but it is difficult to see why considering the scale of some of the earliest examples — particularly those at Crewe and at Swindon. Typically, Brunel's ideas for locomotive sheds were different than those of his contemporaries. At Swindon he designed a running shed, alongside which was the main locomotive shed, nearly 89m long and 43m wide. The 'stalls' for the engines were in rows against each long side wall, and between them running down the centre of the building was a traverser on rails. Locomotives were taken to and from their stalls on the traverser; it was a simple idea but not one that could keep pace with the ever increasing size of locomotives and not one that was copied by other companies.

At Derby, the North Midland Railway built a different type of shed that became one of the standard types in use until the end of steam power. It was designed by Francis Thompson, the architect, as a polygonal building 40m in diameter under a huge wooden roof, supported on cast-iron columns 15m high. Inside were 16 stalls radiating from a central turntable, each stall capable of taking two of the then relatively small locomotives. Opening in 1840, it was the prototype 'roundhouse'.

89   The Roundhouse at Chalk Farm, Camden, was built by the London & Birmingham Railway to replace an earlier shed in 1847. Soon made obsolete by the increasing size of locomotives, for nearly a century it was used as a bonded whisky warehouse. Latterly it has been a theatre.

At the southern end of the London & Birmingham Railway, the original and substantial rectangular locomotive shed was at Camden, on top of the rope-hauled incline down into Euston station. This building was replaced in 1847 by the magnificent roundhouse on Chalk Farm Road that still survives. It was designed by R.B.Dockray with advice from Robert Stephenson, with a huge circular timber roof supported by an internal arcade of cast-iron pillars and brackets; in the middle of the roof was the vent for the smoke, and at track level, a turntable by which the engines could be directed into any of the short lines radiating from it. Unfortunately, locomotives quickly grew in size and within 20 years the roundhouse was too small and was sold; it became a bonded warehouse for nearly a century and was latterly converted into a theatre.

Some companies, such as the Midland and the Great Western, preferred roundhouses for their larger depots whilst others preferred straight sheds. Both had advantages and disadvantages. In a roundhouse, once a locomotive was in its stall it was no longer in the way of any others, but the need for a single entrance line and a turntable could lead to congestion. They were also more expensive to build. Few roundhouses were actually round. Many were polygonal and most were square, the Great Western devising a standard square form of roundhouse by the 1880s. The roundhouse at Inverness was remarkable in being designed rather like a giant doughnut, with a central turntable in the open surrounded by the ring of covered stalls.

90   *Inside the Llanelli roundhouse in 1950; the three locomotives in the stalls were all built for the independent Burry Port & Gwendraeth Valley Railway nearly half a century earlier. Over each stall is a smoke vent.*

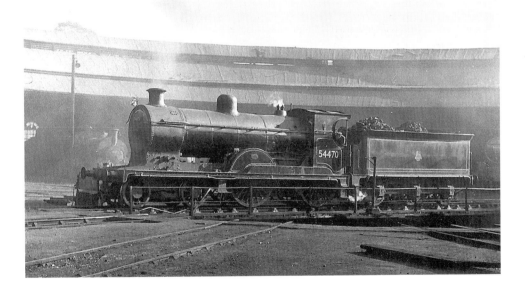

91   *One of the elegant ex-Caledonian Railway 4-4-0s, built in 1916, is turned on the open turntable inside the remarkable Inverness roundhouse in 1957. The locomotives were housed in covered 'stalls' around the centre.*

145

92   *By 1959, standards at most sheds had deteriorated and the end of steam power was in sight —
especially on the Southern Region of British Railways. This is Basingstoke, Hampshire, a
straight shed on the Southern Region.*

Despite their cost, roundhouses were still occasionally built well into the twentieth
century, two very late examples being built in the 1940s. Leicester, opened in 1945,
replaced three older sheds, and Carnforth, Lancashire, is now the centre of Steamtown, a
preservation society.

The straight sheds were always rectangular and generally much easier to build and roof.
Roofs could be large single or multi-pitched structures, although the London & North
Western Railway developed a standard north-light type of roof that could be used for
sheds of virtually any size.

The size and location of sheds depended on several factors. Generally sheds were
needed at or near the main termini; in London, the cost of land and the attitude of the
local authorities generally meant that the sheds were sited a few miles away in the suburbs.
Sheds were also needed at regular intervals along the major routes and at major junctions.
Branch lines were also given sheds as well, as were areas that had heavy goods traffic.
Some sheds could be very large and cater for dozens of locomotives, whilst a branch shed
sometimes was only large enough for one.

Building materials for sheds were as varied as those used for other railway buildings,
though brick became by far the most common material. Some early ones were built of
timber, like the first roundhouse near Paddington on the Great Western, and timber was
also used for less important sheds and by poorer companies throughout the steam era.
Several sheds were timber-framed and covered with corrugated iron sheeting. Early roofs

93   *The Worcester Engine Works was one of several independent companies supplying railway companies in Britain and abroad. This fine polychrome brick building on Shrub Hill Road was erected about 1864, probably designed by Thomas Dickson. The venture was not a success, built only 84 locomotives, and the works closed in 1871 (Ken Hoverd/Archive, 1994).*

94   Wolverton Works, Bedfordshire, became the main carriage building and repair shops on the London & North Western Railway in 1864 and continued to build carriages until the 1960s. Repairs continued thereafter but the works have now been run down. Many of the Victorian buildings survive although most are awaiting new uses. The main line originally went through the middle of the works, past this building, but was diverted to the east.

were generally of timber but iron proved to be more durable and more fire resistant. The last sheds were built in and roofed with reinforced concrete.

All locomotive depots required certain basic facilities, especially those for fuelling and watering the locomotives. Coal was originally loaded by hand into the tenders and this changed very little in some of the smaller and more primitive depots. For most, however, a coal stage was supplied. This was a raised platform reached by a ramp up which a coal waggon could be shunted. The locomotive was pulled up alongside the platform and filled from it — by hand or, later, by semi-automatic machinery. In the twentieth century a handful of the very largest sheds had massive automated coal towers.

Water for the boilers was obviously another vital ingredient at sheds and elsewhere on the rail network. Hundreds of water towers were built, usually consisting of a large iron tank on top of a brick base. Water was pumped into the tank and taken from it by a flexible hose. Other tanks supplied water cranes around the depot or a station.

Steam locomotives also produced waste products, mostly ash and cinder, and these were disposed of at the sheds. Typically ash from the engine's grates was simply dropped into an ash pit dug between the rails. Similar pits, or sometimes the same ones, could be used to inspect the undersides of the locomotive for maintenance purposes.

95   *Water tanks were an important facility at stations and sheds in the days of steam. This one, photographed in 1978, is at Margate station, Kent, which was rebuilt after the local rail system was rationalised by the new Southern Railway in the late 1920s.*

The introduction of diesel and electric locomotives and multiple units in large numbers from the late 1950s, and the closure of lines in the early 1960s, led to the loss of dozens of engine sheds. Both diesel and electric plant required cleaner and brighter conditions than the dirty and dark steam engine sheds, and the closure of lines meant that fewer steam locomotives were needed. The final end of revenue steam-hauled traffic on British Rail in 1968 meant that most of the old MPDs were surplus to requirements. A few of the more modern ones have been adapted for the new order, and some have found new uses. Most, however, have either been demolished or await that fate.

After the pioneering decades of the nineteenth century, locomotives and rolling stock were usually built in purposes built premises. Apart from a handful of locomotives built by the Stockton & Darlington Railway, most railway companies bought locomotives from outside suppliers until the 1840s. Parts of Robert Stephenson's Newcastle works, the first in the world, still survive. This, and later company and private works, were developments of standard heavy engineering factories, pioneered in the eighteenth century by men like Matthew Boulton and James Watt.

The most important of the main railway works included those at Swindon, for the Great Western, Derby, for the Midland, and Crewe, for the London & North Western. As the size of locomotives increased and new techniques were introduced, the works were adapted to meet the new requirements and were constantly being extended and re-equipped. One of the least altered and most intact examples of a purpose built railway works is that built for the Cambrian Railways in 1866 at Oswestry, Shropshire and designed by John Robinson at a cost of £28,000. Though capable of building locomotives it seldom did so and was mainly a maintenance depot for locomotives and rolling stock. Little altered physically, it closed nearly a hundred years after it opened and now houses a variety of commercial premises. An overall plan is needed to ensure its long-term future.

Whilst some works concentrated on the construction and major repairs to and of locomotives, others were dedicated to other types of rolling stock. In major centres, such as Derby and Swindon, the locomotive and carriage departments were part of the same site. A few other works specialised in rolling stock. Wolverton, for example, had originally been the main works for both locomotives and carriage repairs on the London & Birmingham Railway but was subsequently made into the London & North Western's main carriage building and repair centre, a role that continued into the 1980s. There were also several purpose built carriage sheds built in the nineteenth century at main line termini and at major junctions. Early carriages were made of wood and other vulnerable materials and were not as hardy as the later steel bodied vehicles.

13 Signal boxes

Waggonways and plateways had no need of anything but the most rudimentary signalling systems. Speeds were, literally, walking pace and an individual waggon or train could easily stop if there was a problem on the line. Many of the routes were double tracked, but even where there was only a single line, head-on collisions were few — though there may have been the occasional dispute over the right of way.

The advent of steam power hardly changed matters at first. Speeds were still slow and traffic light, and it was simply left up to the engine drivers to keep a good look out at the way ahead. It quickly became apparent that a more sophisticated method of train safety was needed and an *ad hoc* system of hand and flag signals led quickly to the use of proper permanent indicators and signals, especially at stations and junctions. A wide variety of different signals were used, including discs, lamps, flags, signs, and balls being raised, lowered, or turned; 'kite' signals were pieces of canvas stretched onto a frame and, when spread, meant danger, and when furled, 'proceed'.

The first semaphore signal on a railway, copying the well-established coastal communications system — such as that between Portsmouth and London — was installed in 1841 on the London & Croydon Railway at its junction with the London & Greenwich Railway in New Cross Gate by the company's engineer, Charles Gregory. The signals had three positions — hidden in the post slot meant 'line clear'; at right-angles to the post meant 'danger'; and 45 degrees meant caution. Three position semaphores were not widely adopted or that common, despite a brief revival before and after the First World War, and varieties of simpler two position designs evolved instead.

All of these early signals were worked by hand, mostly by the railway companies' policemen. The first signal boxes were literally trackside sheds in which the policemen could shelter. As signals became more numerous and more widespread, especially as the increasing speed of trains led to the need for warning, or 'distant' signals well away from the 'home' signal close to the policeman's cabin, the use of wires or bars to control the signals became more common. By concentrating the controls for the signals in one place the time taken to operate them was reduced and the policemen could concentrate simply on the signals — thus becoming specialist signalmen. At around the same time the hand-operation of points also gave way to lever and wire and could be operated from the same place as the signals; the pointsmen thus also became signalmen.

96 *A typical nineteenth century signal box, probably of the 1880s, at Tram Inn south of Hereford on the former Newport, Abergavenny & Hereford Railway. The name is a reminder of the former horse-drawn tramway that the railway company had to buy out to make their new line.*

Although the signals and points could be operated from the same place, there were still no connections between them and the facilities were still very basic. The levers were either on a raised platform or, at major junctions or stations, on a gantry over the tracks. They were still in the open and the huts were still used as shelters rather than anything else. This soon changed after the development of 'interlocking'. Up until then it was possible to mistakenly have signals showing a train that the line ahead was clear whilst other signals or the points were against it. By mechanically connecting individual signals and then points and signals, such potentially perilous mistakes could be prevented.

The first attempt to interlock signals was by Gregory at the Bricklayers Arms junction on the London & Croydon Railway in 1843 and points and signals were first interconnected on the Manchester, Sheffield & Lincolnshire Railway's junction at East Retford in 1852. Improvements were rapidly made; in 1856 John Saxby of the London Brighton & South Coast Railway patented his 'Simultaneous Motion' suitable for simple junctions, and in 1860 Austin Chambers of the North London Railway patented a much improved system — described as the 'Successive Motion' — capable of being used at the most complex junctions and first used at the Kentish Town junction on the NLR. These developments did mean that the equipment became more complicated, more expensive, and took up more space.

97   *Woburn Sands signal box, Bedfordshire, has the typical composite construction of a brick lower floor containing the locking room and a weatherboarded upper floor. It is beginning to show its age.*

The earliest interlocked signal boxes were usually built of timber and consisted of a raised covered platform at the level of the operating levers above the rods and shafts, which were left open to the elements. From the early 1860s a distinctly improved and long-lived design emerged. The more complicated interlocking mechanism below the platform became a full storey in its own right and it became sensible for the companies to protect their expensive apparatus. The open framework below the platform was covered, initially by weatherboarding. In a very short time, some companies began to build this lower part of their boxes — which became known as the *locking room* — in brick or, in some areas, stone.

Conditions for the signalmen improved dramatically with the provision of an all-over roof to the former open platform, which now evolved into a proper *operating floor*. A fireplace was now usually provided for the signalmen as well. Large opening windows on the track side and ends of the operating floor became a distinctive feature of the signal boxes, as were the external steps leading up to the platform floor (there seldom being space within the locking room). The basic design of the signal box changed very little until the 1920s. Most were two-storey and built in brick or timber, or had a brick base and a timber top. Stone was used where it was locally and cheaply available. The roofs were usually slate-covered and either hipped or gable-ended — the latter design allowing for

98   *The Severn Bridge Junction signal box, opened in 1903, is the largest surviving manual signal box in the country although many of the levers in this 1985 view of the interior are no longer used. Under threat of demolition for many years, it has now become a 'listed' building because of its historical importance.*

some decoration in the bargeboards. The locking rooms were originally well-lit, to aid maintenance of the mechanism, but a large number of windows were later blocked up during the Second World War as part of air-raid precautions.

Most railway companies designed their own signal boxes and developed a specific house style; others were content to buy in from the larger manufacturers of signalling contractors who generally supplied the mechanisms; the three main British companies were Stevens & Co., Saxby & Farmer, and McKenzie & Holland. Most boxes were built to fairly standard designs but there were cases where this was not possible or desirable. Difficult restricted sites required narrower or taller boxes. Particularly busy junctions could require a signal box to be built on a gantry over the tracks, and some busy stations had secondary boxes built on their platforms. By far the worst of all were the few boxes built inside tunnels — these included those of the late-1860s on the Metropolitan Railway, one just outside St. Pancras station opened in 1890, two on the Mersey Railway of 1892, and another opened in the early 1900s in the Woodhead Tunnel under the Pennines.

Signal boxes were one of the most numerous of railway structures. They were sited at stations, junctions, goods yards, sidings and level crossings and there were probably over

13,000 of them in existence before the First World War. Changes to them were generally few, as the interlocking systems proved remarkably long-lasting and there was seldom any need to alter something that was still functioning properly. If major changes were made and a new box was needed, it was more common to replace the old one entirely than to try and enlarge it — although there are recorded cases of minor extensions to old boxes.

Their longevity meant that there was little need for replacement boxes and huge numbers of mid-Victorian signal boxes remained in use well into the 1960s — and many still do. This in turn means that relatively few signal boxes were built that reflected changing architectural styles. The best examples of 'modern' boxes were built by the Southern Railway in the 1930s, with bold curves and brick and concrete detailing echoing the new cinemas of the time. Most other modern boxes by the 'Big Four', and latterly by British Railways, have tended to be far more utilitarian.

Developments in 'power signalling' and the use of electrics in all aspects of signalling — from the interlocking to colour signals — were surprisingly slow to replace the traditional mechanical signal box. Colour signals had been introduced as early as 1898 on underground lines — on the Waterloo & City Railway — and above ground on the Liverpool Overhead Railway in 1920. By 1938 there were 3000 coloured light signals in use on the lines of the 'Big Four'. The war slowed the changeover so that by the time the railways were nationalised in 1948 there were about 5000. This had increased to about 9000 by 1955 when the Modernisation Plan came into force which recommended the elimination of the old semaphore signals. At that time there were still nearly 10,000 signal boxes in use.

The massive line closures of the 1960s, the decay in pick-up freight traffic and the subsequent loss of marshalling yards and sidings, the introduction of continental-style automated level-crossings, and further improvements in signalling technology allowing large fully electronic 'panel' boxes to control numerous sections of track making smaller signal boxes obsolete, all led to a rapid decrease in their numbers. By 1970 there were about 4,000 left and by the year 2000 there will be less than a thousand. Computer technology and advanced electronics have concentrated most signalling into major 'Signalling Centres'. One of the earliest of these, at Motherwell, opened in 1973 and made 67 mechanical signal boxes redundant at a stroke. The busiest of these new facilities is the Trent Signalling Centre and there are also three in the London area — at Clapham Junction, London Bridge, and Victoria.

Curiously, delays in converting fully to coloured light signals meant that mechanical boxes were still occasionally being built until the start of the 1980s. The largest mechanical box remaining, Shrewsbury Severn Bridge, built after the station was enlarged in 1903, has been under threat for the past 30 years; it has 180 levers (mostly unused) controlling points and lower-quadrant semaphore signals of old Great Western Railway — even though it was built by the London & North Western Railway.

14 Miscellany

Large numbers of other buildings were built by the railway companies for all sorts of reasons. Often paternalistic, several companies built houses for their workers and some built whole suburbs or towns. The commonest domestic building, excluding the stationmaster's house, was the crossing-keeper's cottage. Railways were obliged, in the steam railway age, to make sure that level crossing gates were manned. Level crossing had existed on waggonways and tramways and usually did not need gates other than those needed to prevent livestock getting onto the tracks and ending up trapped between the fences alongside them. A few of the busier and larger tramways did have manned crossings, sometimes with a shelter for the gatekeeper.

Oddly, the earliest steam railways were allowed to close the gates against the road rather than against their rails. This was made law by the 1839 Highways Act which also forced railway companies to man their crossings. Manning crossings, especially if night traffic was envisaged, led to the provision of cottages next to them for the keepers. These provided reasonable accommodation and, being tied to their employment, reasonably well-behaved and conscientious gatekeepers. Architecturally they often mirrored the station buildings, if there were any nearby, but were usually significantly smaller. Many companies merely provided small brick bungalows.

Once signal boxes had become established, most crossings could be operated by the signal man. On quieter lines this may simply have meant the signal man leaving the box to manually operate the gates, or one of the station porters could do the same thing. On busier lines and later, on most, the crossing gates could be operated by rods from the signal box itself. The crossing keepers' cottages, although seldom now needed to house a crossing keeper, were generally retained by the companies to house other employees.

The traditional level crossing gates made of timber, and later iron, changed very little from the 1840s onwards for over a century. Light Railways did not need gates, incidentally. The continental 'barber's pole' barrier appeared first on military railways, particularly those taken over in the Second World War, but were manually operated. The first fully-automatic level crossing with raising barriers was installed at Spath Crossing on the former North Staffordshire Railway's Churnet Valley branch near Uttoxeter in 1961; the line closed four years later.

99   *The most basic of level crossings was still in use near Silvertown in London's Docklands in the mid-1980s. The hut for the keeper to shelter in would have been almost identical to those built for crossing keepers and signal men almost 150 years earlier.*

In the more remote areas companies also provided trackside houses for other employees, such as signalmen and platelayers and there were often groups of such houses clustered around isolated stations. By default, railway companies became town planners as well. Several towns were established or considerably enlarged by the creation of major railway depots. The first three of these were all placed roughly midway along major trunk railways. The London & Birmingham set up their works at Wolverton, midway between those two towns, in 1838; the Grand Junction moved its main works from Liverpool to Crewe, at a junction by a hamlet midway between Birmingham and Manchester, in 1840; and the Great Western established their main locomotive and carriage works at Swindon in 1841. All three companies provided reasonably good quality cottages for their workers, usually in terraces, and better houses for the managers and foremen. Churches, chapels and institutes were usually provided or part-financed by, the companies. In well-established towns, the railway companies developed virtually self-contained villages, such as around the Midland Railway headquarters in Derby.

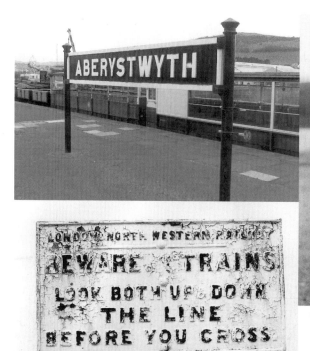

100-5 The railways needed thousands of signs of all different types, and many are still in use years later. Unfortunately, the enthusiasm for railway memorabilia had led to their value increasing and becoming targets for thieves. Cast-iron signs are particularly sought-after and so particularly vulnerable.

106   *A mile post on a disused line.*

107   *A London & North Western Railway bridge plate.*

108   *A level crossing plate.*

Glossary

Abutment The solid part of a pier or end wall of an approach embankment from which the bridge span begins. Often flanked by wing walls (q.v.).

Accommodation bridge Bridge built over or under the line to link separate parts of farm or estate cut by the railway.

Accommodation crossing Private unmanned level crossing linking separate parts of a farm or estate cut by the railway, usually fitted with gates or stiles.

Air Shaft Vertical shaft from surface level to tunnel below, usually one of the original working shafts that was retained and often topped by a small tower or turret.

Atmospheric railway A railway powered by a piston underneath the rolling stock inside a tube between the rails. As air is pumped out in front of the piston by stationary steam engines along the line a vacuum is created and the train moves forward. Used in particular by Brunel in South Devon but proved too complex and unreliable.

Automatic crossing Level crossing operated automatically on the approach of a train, usually with barriers on the continental pattern.

AWS Automatic Warning System, introduced to give train drivers a signal in their cabs warning about signals and capable of applying brakes if caution signals are ignored.

Ballast	Infill between and under track sleepers to keep track rigid and to prevent is slipping. Usually of crushed stone but broken slag, ash, pebbles and clay have all been used as well.
Bascule bridge	Type of drawbridge occasionally used on railways, especially those crossing navigable rivers or on harbour branches.
Barlow rail	Type of bridge rail patented in 1849 by William Barlow capable of being spiked directly to the ballast and needing no sleepers. Based on Brunel's bridge rail.
Barrier crossing	Continental type of level crossing with lifting barriers rather than gates; usually worked automatically.
Battery	Eighteenth century North-east England term for an embankment.
Bay (Platform)	Shorter platform with buffer stop(s) typically built into a longer and wider platform of a through station and used for local branch trains. Generally taking one line of track but sometimes two.
Bay track	Track leading to a bay platform.
Beeching Report	Report on British Railways by committee chaired by Dr Richard Beeching published as *The Reshaping of British Railways* in 1963. It led to the closure of many branch, and some main, lines. Also referred to as the Beeching Axe.
Big Four, the	In 1923 most railway companies were amalgamated within four regional groups — the Great Western, the London, Midland & Scottish, the London & North Eastern, and the Southern Railways. These lasted until Nationalisation in 1948.
Birkinshaw rail	Earliest successful wrought iron rails, I-sectioned, and developed in 1820 by John Birkinshaw
Block system	Signalling system widely adopted on British railways that divides lengths of track into 'blocks' that only one train at a time can enter; all controlled by signal boxes at either end of the block.
Booking Office	Part of station from which tickets are purchased.

Board of Trade	Government body responsible for monitoring all aspects of railway safety from 1840 until 1919 when the Ministry of Transport was created. All lines had to be passed by BoT inspectors before being opened and all accidents were also investigated by them.
Bow-string bridge	Type of metal bridge truss in which the feet of the main arch are joined by a tie-beam at track level, creating a self-contained structural unit.
Branch line	Secondary line off a larger one, sometimes a dead-end.
Bridge rail	Type of rail with a section like an upside down 'U', usually of wrought iron and used extensively by Brunel on the GWR Broad gauge.
Broad gauge	Name applied to any line with a gauge greater than the Standard gauge of 4ft $8\frac{1}{2}$in, but often meaning the 7ft $0\frac{1}{4}$ in of Brunel.
Bull-headed rail	I-section wrought iron or steel rail with the top section slightly thicker than the base. Used as standard rail on standard gauge British railways from about the 1840s until 1949 and still used on some cross-country lines and the London Underground.
Carriage shed	Large building with through tracks in which to store and maintain carriages; usually situated near the ends of main lines or at major junctions.
Cantenary	The supporting cables for the conductor wire in overhead electric lines.
Cattle creep	Low and narrow occupation underbridge built to allow access for livestock to fields separated by the railway.
Chair	Shoe, usually cast-iron, fixed to sleeper, into which the rail is slotted and fixed in place by a wooden or steel key.
Chair bolts	Bolts to fix the chairs (q.v.) to the sleepers.
Check rail	Additional rail inside the running rail to assist keeping the wheels on the track at cross-overs, points, curves, viaducts, etc.
Chord	The top and bottom members of a latticed or trussed girder.

Cliff railway	Steeply inclined cable-hauled railway, often self-acting and usually built for pleasure traffic at coastal resorts — though a handful were built inland.
Clip	Steel sprung clip fixing flat-bottomed rails in place on modern track.
Coal stage	Platform, usually in the locomotive depot, used to store coal ready to be loaded into the locomotive tender.
Coal winder	Large automated coal loading apparatus used on only the largest railway locomotive depots from the 1930s onwards.
Container terminal	Road/rail interchange sidings where containers are transferred from road lorries to container wagons. Also rail/port interchange served by container ships. Modern version Freightliners introduced in 1963.
Crossing loop	Double tracked section on otherwise single line allowing trains to pass.
Crossover (road)	Rail link between two or more parallel lines of track.
Culvert	Small drain, usually brick lined, underneath the tracks carrying a drainage ditch, small stream, etc.
Cut and cover	Method of constructing shallow tunnels by first excavating a cutting and then roofing it over. Used on the higher underground lines in London for example.
Cut and fill	General method of using spoil excavated from cuttings on a line under construction in the embankments.
Cutting	Excavation through high ground to take the line through at a steady gradient. The angle of slope depends on the rock strata or soil. In urban areas usually with vertical masonry walls to save on space.
Decking	The flooring of a girder bridge, usually timber but later iron or steel.
Depot	Early name for railway stations (passenger or goods) in Britain and used more commonly in North America.

Diamond crossover	Crossing of two lines on the diagonal, forming a lozenge shape in plan (see also Single and Double compounds).
Distant signal	First signal in a set of signals guarding a block (q.v.). In semaphores, usually yellow with a cut out 'V' at the end and a black V across it.
Double compound	Type of diamond crossover where it is also possible to change from both tracks to the other (see diamond crossover and single compound).
Double-headed rail	Iron rail of balanced I section designed so that once one side has been worn it can be turned over until the other side is worn as well. The theory was better than the practise.
Double track	Line of railway with two lines of track, one for each direction.
Down	The direction of most routes used to be referred to as being 'up' or 'down' rather than geographic. 'Down' usually meant down from London or from another major centre.
Dram road	Alternate eighteenth century term for Tramroad, waggonway, etc.
Embankment	Linear earthwork built as part of the foundation level to carry railway over valleys and lower ground.
Facing points	Points 'facing' approaching trains.
Fish-bellied rails	Early form of cast-iron or wrought-iron rails with deliberate swollen convex soffits designed for strength.
Fish-bolt	Bolt to connect pairs of fish-plates (q.v.).
Fish-plate	Pair of plates joined together by bolts through the adjoining ends of rails forming a coupling without interfering with the wheels. Patented by William Adams in 1847.
Flanged wheel	Wheel with outer, thinner, rim extension designed to keep it on the rails.
Flat-bottomed rail	Rail with a flattened lower section that could be fixed directly to the sleepers. Early examples devised by Charles Vignolles in England but not main line British standard until 1949.

Flying Junction/Flyover	Overbridge carrying a branch line over a main line to avoid interfering with the traffic on either. Expensive and rare.
Formation level	The level created by the earthworks and bridges of a railway, ready to take the Permanent Way (q.v.).
Gangroad	Old English East Midlands term for waggonway.
Gauge	The distance between the paired rails of track.
Girder	Horizontal structural members — in railway context, of a bridge. Usually timber or metal. (see latticed g-; plate-g-.)
Goods line/branch	Line used purely for goods traffic (see also Mineral line)
Gradient	The slope of a section of railway. The ruling gradient is the steepest on a particular line or branch.
Gradient post	Trackside sign indicating the direction and angle of a gradient; usually the gradient is shown as 1 in 500, etc. Signs were in wood, iron or concrete.
Green	Colour on semaphore and electric signals indicating that the line ahead is clear.
Ground frame	Small signal and/or points frame away from a signal box, usually unprotected from the weather but still interlocked with the main signal block.
Ground signal/disc	Miniature signal used in sidings, etc.
Grouping	The amalgamations forming the Big Four (q.v.) in 1923.
Halt	Small station, usually unstaffed and often with primitive amenities. Many created in the 1920s and 30s in an effort to boost traffic. Often built of wood.
Hogged, or Hog-backed	Girder, plate or latticed, with distinct segmental profile to its top member or chord, designed to add additional increasing strength to the central sections.
Home signal	Signal controlling entry into a block (q.v.), usually red with a white bar. Sometimes there are outer and inner home signals.

Horse-drawn	Railway or plateway using horses for motive power.
Hump yard	Marshalling yard in which shunting can be carried out by gravity by building a rising gradient and allowing individual wagons to roll down from the top into the required siding.
Hybrid railway	Term coined to describe railways that were neither all horse-drawn nor entirely locomotive drawn — particularly those built at the dawn of the steam age that included such things as rope-haulage.
Interlocking	The system whereby signals and points are interlinked to avoid errors.
Inverted arch	The shallow upside down segmental arch at the bottom of a tunnel bore under the permanent way. Sometimes also used in brick-lined cuttings if the ground is particularly unstable.
Jig; Jigger	Shropshire term for the primitive brake used on waggonways; the jigger was the brakeman.
Joint	The gap between adjoining rails; it has to be altered to allow for contraction or expansion at different times of year.
Jubilee track	Light flat-bottomed iron railed track designed to be easily portable and suited to war and industrial use where lines were not intended to stay permanently in one place.
Key	Block of wood or steel spring holding a rail in place in a chair (q.v.).
Kyanising	Pioneering form of preserving timbers for sleepers or bridges developed by J. H. Kyan in the 1830s. Timbers were immersed in bi-chloride of mercury.
Latticed girder	Open trussed girder structure, usually wrought iron or steel, with top and bottom members (chords) linked by others. (see e.g. Pratt truss, and Warren truss).
Lengthman's hut	Lineside hut for track maintenance personnel. Lines were divided into 'lengths' each looked after by a single gang and each length usually had its own hut. Mostly of brick, though earlier ones are of timber. Some were heated.

Light railway	Railway built under the auspices of the Light Railway Act of 1896 which allowed them to be less well built than main lines providing speed was restricted and special arrangements made at level crossings, etc. Also refers to other non-main line track in general.
Loading gauge	The size limits, height and width, for rolling stock on a railway. Also a metal or wooden frame over the track indicating these dimensions. If a train fails to clear it, it cannot use the line.
Loop	Siding connected at either end to the running line. On single track lines the loops were often at the stations.
Lower quadrant signal	A semaphore signal that drop downwards when it is off and the line is clear.
Marshalling yard	Sidings in which trains are made up or 'marshalled' by shunting wagons around. Larger ones have arrival, shunting, and departure sidings. 'Flat' yards are worked entirely by shunting engines. 'Gravity' or 'Hump' yards are graded and can be worked partially without (see 'hump').
Memel pine	Good quality deal from the Baltic, extensively used in railway construction in the mid-nineteenth century.
Metals	Slang name for the rails.
Miniature railway	Technically, any railway with a gauge of less than 2ft and designed for recreation rather than industrial use.
Mixed gauge	Railways in which two different gauges can work by the introduction of a third rail. Now rare but quite common in some areas in the nineteenth century before the elimination of the Broad gauge (q.v.).
MPD	Initials for Motive Power Depot, a term for engine sheds introduced in the mid-twentieth century.
Narrow gauge	Any railway with a gauge smaller than the Standard gauge of 4ft 8½in.
Navvy	General term for construction worker building the railways in the nineteenth century. Used for canal builders too and derived from 'navigator'.

Newcastle Road	Term used in North-east England for waggonway.
Occupation bridge	Over or underbridge between fields or estate separated by the railway but not necessarily taking a lane or track. For use by the owner or tenant only.
Occupation crossing	Level crossing, usually only of planks guarded by kissing gates, allowing access to fields divided by the railway. for use by the owner or tenant only.
Opening up	The conversion of a shallow tunnel into a cutting.
Overbridge	A bridge over a railway, carrying a road, track, canal, or another railway. Opposite to underbridge (q.v.).
Overhead electric	A system of electrification in which the power is taken from overhead wires slung between gantries.
Parapet	In bridges, the rails or balustrade.
Permanent Way	The track and ballast laid on top of the Formation level (q.v.) once the line is ready for opening, as distinct from the temporary contractors track.
Pier	In bridges, the intermediate support for the arches or girders.
Plate girder	Iron or steel girder made up of several plates of iron or steel riveted or welded together.
Plateway	Tramway using L-sectioned rails, usually of cast-iron, and flangeless wheels. Introduced in the late eighteenth century.
Platform	Raised masonry or timber structure at stations and goods depots to help access to and from trains.
Points	Short moveable sections of track designed to allow trains to change from one line to another. Developed by the eighteenth century on wooden waggonways.
Pratt truss	Type of trussed latticed girder in which there are both vertical and diagonal members between the top and bottom chords. Sometimes known as an 'N-truss'.

Private siding	Railway siding dedicated to one customer, usually commercial, and not for general use.
Railroad	Eighteenth and early nineteenthth century British term for railways that became widespread in North America.
Rails	The parallel members on which railway rolling stock runs; they are now generally of iron or steel but were also of wood.
Railway Mania(s)	Period of frenzied speculation in railway construction in the 1840s, peaking in 1845. Led to many failed schemes. A second lesser mania occurred in the early 1860s.
Reception sidings	Sidings in which goods trains can be accommodated away from running lines to await sorting in the marshalling yard (q.v.).
Refuge	Recess in tunnel lining or bridge parapet for lengthsmens' safety when trains pass.
Refuge Siding	Siding in which goods trains can leave the main line to let a passenger train past.
Ring	In a brick arch, one of the 'rings' of brick making up the structure of the arch — hence two-ring, three-ring, four-ring arches, etc.
Route mileage	The distance of the route of a particular line or system, as opposed to Track Mileage (q.v.).
Running shed	Small locomotive depot with limited facilities serving a small area of track or a branch line.
Scissors crossing	Double track crossover.
Self-acting plane	A railed incline on which one wagon travelling in the down direction helps to haul another in the up direction by means of gravity, the two being connected by a rope wound around a braked drum at the top. Usually with two rails of track, occasionally with one and a passing loop midway.
Semaphore signal	Old-fashioned form of signal consisting an arm pivoting on a post. In all forms when the bar is horizontal, the signal is 'on' and trains must stop. Variants include upper and lower quadrant, and somersault.

Shed	Common name for a locomotive depot
Siding	A section of track used to store, load, or marshall trains or separate pieces of rolling stock.
Signal	Visible indicator of the state of the line ahead for the train driver. Developed into semaphore signals and later coloured light signals.
Signal box	Building from which the signals, points and level crossing gates are operated.
Signal gantries	Iron or iron and timber structures over the track supporting two or many more signals depending on the number of lines and junctions.
Single compound	Type of diamond crossover in which it is also possible to move from one line to another but not vice versa (see diamond crossover and double compound).
Single track	A railway with just one line of track used by trains travelling in both directions — but not at the same time.
Sleeper	Support for rails laid in ballast. Timber sleepers were used from the seventeenth century, cast-iron ones were tried in the late eighteenth, and stone blocks were popular in the early nineteenth before transverse timber sleepers became standard from the 1840s. Concrete and steel sleepers have been developed since the 1950s.
Somersault signal	Type of semaphore signal in which the signal arm does not pivot on the post but on the end of a short bracket instead. Signal at 'danger' (or 'on') is horizontal. Drop down to vertical when 'off'. Never very common.
Sorting siding	Main sidings in a marshalling yard (q.v.) in which individual wagons are sorted and coupled into trains.
Span	The gap between piers or abutments of a bridge.
Spandrel	In a bridge, that portion between the arch and the parapet.
Springing	The point at which an arch begins, or 'springs'.

Staggered platforms	Stations in which the two platforms are not directly opposite each other. This may because of the terrain or several other factors.
Staithe	Staging, usually timber, by a wharf, on which waggons could be unloaded directly into the waiting barges or ships.
Standard gauge	The normal gauge in Britain and throughout much of the world of 4ft 8½in.
Station	Complex for loading and unloading passengers and/or goods.
Stationary steam engine	Fixed engine, usually housed in an engine shed and served by a boiler house or houses; in railway use usually designed to operate rope haulage, especially on inclines. Also used for the Atmospheric railways (q.v.) and, for general use, in railway works, etc.
Swing bridge	Bridge that pivots on a central axis that can be opened to allow passage by ships or barges. Occasionally used on railways crossing navigable rivers or canals.
Temporary way	Temporary track used during construction or sometimes repair of the railway.
Third-rail electric	Electric system in which power is taken from a third rail between or next to the main carrying rails.
Ticket platform	Platform outside the main stations formerly used as an alternate drop-off point for passengers and a place to check on tickets.
Tilt	The degree to which the rails are tilted slightly in towards each other by the chair seating, usually at an angle of 1 in 20.
Track	General term for the rails, sleepers, chairs, ballast, etc., on which the trains run.
Track Mileage	The length of the total length of tracks on a system, including double lines, sidings, etc., as opposed to Route Mileage (q.v.)
Trailing points	Points leading away from an approaching train — i.e. to use them the train would have to reverse.

Train ferry   Ship or boat ferry capable of taking railway rolling stock across rivers or on longer distances without the need to tranship. They have railway lines on their decks. First examples across the Firth of Forth in 1849. First cross-Channel ferries were started during the First World War for military traffic from Richborough, Kent, to France.

Tramway   General name for a plateway in the late-eighteenth and early nineteenth century, as opposed to waggonway or railway.

Tramroad   Alternate name for Tramway (q.v.).

Tube   Slang name for the London Underground lines.

Tunnel   Subterranean passage cut through a hill to take a railway, or a covered 'cut-and-cover' cutting (q.v.).

Turnrail   Obsolete word for a small waggonway turntable.

Turntable   Short rotating section of track on which rolling stock can be turned around. Used especially for locomotives but in early days of steam railways also for wagons and coaches.

Underbridge   A bridge under the railway, .i.e. the railway goes over the bridge — typical examples being river bridges and viaducts.

Up   Opposite direction to Down (q.v.), usually meant up to London or another major centre or junction.

Upper quadrant   A semaphore signal that rises upwards to about 45° when it is 'off' and the line is clear. Standard on all but the GWR system by the late 1920s.

Viaduct   Longer underbridge usually carrying the railway across a broad geographical feature such as a wide valley, or through a built up area.

Vignoles rail   Flat bottomed rail developed by Charles Vignoles in the late 1830s.

Voussoirs   In an arch, the wedge shaped stones or bricks making up the structure.

Waggonway	Early form of railway, with wooden rails and sleepers; usually gravity or horse powered.
Waiting Room	Room in a station for passengers. Formerly segregated at some by class or even sex.
Warren truss	Type of latticed girder first used in 1848 by James Warren and one that became very popular for all types of wrought iron and steel railway bridges. The top and bottom chords (q.v.) are linked by crossing diagonal members.
Water crane	Lineside apparatus designed to provide water for steam locomotives at stations or depots.
Water troughs	Very long but very shallow troughs laid between the rails to allow steam locomotives to fill up their water tanks without having to stop. First introduced by water troughs invented by John Ramsbottom of the LNWR in 1859 and used at Mochdre on the Chester-Holyhead line.
Wayleave	Old term for a right of passage, informal or formal, over other people's land; became an important part of establishing the early waggonway routes.
Wing wall	Walls often flanking the abutments of bridges, especially where there are approach embankments. Wing walls usually are at an angle to the main abutment and slope down with the embankment profile.
Woodenway	Another name for a waggonway (q.v.).

Gazetteer

For obvious reasons, this gazetteer can only be very selective. It attempts to list some of the more important sites as well as some more typical ones, but there will inevitably be some ommisions due to lack of space. The listed bridges and stations are particularly selective, as, despite closure and demolition, good quality ones survive in very large numbers. It must be emphasised that some of these sites are in private hands and on private land.

Key

GJR	Grand Junction Railway
L&BR	London & Birmingham Railway
L&MR	Liverpool & Manchester Railway
L&NWR	London & North Western Railway
L&SWR	London & South Western Railway
LBSCR	London, Brighton & South Coast Railway
LMS	London, Midland & Scottish Railway
OW&WR	Oxford, Worcester & Wolverhampton Railway
S&BR	Shrewsbury & Birmingham Railway
S&CR	Shrewsbury & Chester Railway
S&DR	Stockton & Darlington Railway
S&HR	Shrewsbury & Hereford Railway
SA&MR	Sheffield, Ashton-under-Lyne & Manchester Railway
SURC	Shropshire Union of Railways & Canals

Early Remains

The following are specific surviving features of the early railways but there are also several reasonably well-preserved stretches of long abandoned routes that include earthworks, occasional bridges, and runs of stone sleeper blocks. Amongst the best of these are the Penydarren Tramroad south of Merthyr Tydfill and the Hirwaun to Abernant line, both Mid-Glamorgan; the Silkstone Railway, South Yorkshire; the Ticknall Tramroad and the Peak Forest Tramroad, Derbyshire; and the Parker Fell waggonway, Cumbria.

Alloa, Central	Waggonway bridges, 1766	NS 884 927 & NS 886 929
Alloa, Central	Waggonway tunnel, 1766	NT 886928
Beckley Burn, Co. Durham	Waggonway embankment or 'battery', 1720s	NZ 204561
Brampton Sands, Cumbria	Weigh-house on Brampton Railway, c.1775	NY 550600
Buxworth Basin, Derbyshire	Canal/tramroad interchange, B Outram, c.1796S	
		K 020821
Chapel Milton, Derbyshire	Tunnel on Peak Forest Tramway, B Outram, 1796	
		SK 058816
Crickheath, Shropshire	Canal/tramroad interchange, c.1790s	SJ 292234
Froghall, Staffordshire	Canal/tramroad interchange, 1777 and later	SK 028476
Hirwaun, Mid-Glam	Stone-walled tramroad causeway, G Overton, 1808	
		SN 958057
Ironbridge, Shropshire	Dale End plateway warehouse & wharf, c.1830	
		SJ 667 036
Irvine, Strathclyde	Four-arch stone tramroad river bridge, 1811	NS 383369
Monkwray Brow, Cumbria	Earthworks of Parker waggonway, c.1738	NX 969167
Newdale, Shropshire	Stone and brick waggonway bridge, c.1760	SJ 676095
Merthyr Tydfil, Mid-Glam	Pontycafnau, an iron tramroad bridge, c.1793	
		SO 038071
Purley, Surrey	Relaid Surrey Iron Railway track, c.1802	TQ 316622
Robertstown, Mid-Glam	Iron tramroad bridge over Afon Cynon, 1811	SN 997036
Straford-on-Avon, Warwks.	Brick viaduct, Stratford & Moreton R., 1826	SP 205548
Tanfield, Tyneside	Causey Arch, stone waggonway bridge, 1720s	
		NZ 201559
Ticknall, Derbyshire	Stone and brick tramroad underbridge, c.1802	
		SK 356240
Ticknall, Derbyshire	Tramroad tunnels, c.1802	SK 352232
		& SK 356237
Tondu, Mid-Glam	Glan-rhyd bridge, Bridgend R., J Hodgkinson, 1829	
		SS 898828
Whitfield, Tyneside	Waggonway earthworks at High Spen, early C18th	
		NZ 137596

Major Earthworks

Every single line created earthworks of varying size and even some of the minor railways have left a legacy of tall embankments and deep cuttings. The following list is therefore only a small and hopefully representative sample of some of the more significant.

Bath, Avon	Sydney Gardens, stone-lined; GWR, Brunel, 1841
	ST 760652
Belper, Derbyshire	Stone-lined cuttings, N. Midland R, 1840 SK 349475
Roade, Northamptonshire	22m deep cutting, L&BR, R Stephenson, 1838
	SP 750525
Rugby, Warwickshire	1½ mile straight embankment, L&BR, 1838 SP 535745
Sonning, Berkshire	Cutting, 2 miles long; GWR, I K Brunel, 1841
	SU 759744
Talerdigg, Powys	38m deep cutting, Newtown & Machynlleth,1863
	SH 928006
Tring, Hertfordshire	2½ mile cutting, L&BR, R Stephenson, 1838
	SP 940137

Inclines

Inclines, or inclined planes, formed some of the earliest major earthworks on pre-steam railways and then first demonstrated the possible use of steam power for railed transport. They were important elements of the hybrid railways being built until the 1830's, and continued to be used for industrial purposes.

Bagworth, Leicestershire	Leicester & Swannington, R Stephenson, 1832
	SK 446090
Coalport, Shropshire	Hay; Shropshire Canal incline, H Williams, 1792
	SJ 695 028
Glynneath, West Glam	Early powered tramroad incline, 1803-5 SN 891064
Middleton Top, Derbyshire	Cromford & High Peak R., 1831 SK 275552
Morwellham, Cornwall	Tavistock Canal, 1817 SX 447696
Nantmawr, Shropshire	Potteries, Shrewsbury & North Wales R., c.1866
	SJ 253245
Newtyle, Tayside	Dundee & Newtyle R., 1831 NO 299413
Preston, Lancs.	Avenham incline, Lancaster Canal tramroad, c.1803
	SD 542287
Shildon, Co. Durham	Brusselton incline, Stockton & Darlington R., 1825
	NZ 211256
Ynysmeudy, West Glam.	On Cwm Nant Llwd tramroad, 1828 SN 737046

Bridges

Bridges are one of the most common types of railway structures; there were probably around 100,000 bridge points on British railways and a surprisingly high proportion of these survive long after the lines have closed. The following list is only a short selection of some of the more notable.

Arley, Worcestershire	Severn Valley R., J Fowler, 1862	
		SO 767792
Aultnaslanach, Highland	Timber viaduct, Highland Railway, 1897	NH 760349
Balcombe, West Sussex	Ouse; London & Brighton R, J Raistrick, 1841	
		TO 323278
Ballochmyle, Strathclyde	Glasgow, Paisley, Kilmarnock & Ayr R., 1848	
		NS 508254
Barmouth, Gwynedd	Timber; Cambrian Railways, T Savin, 1865-6	
		SH 622151
Berwick-upon-Tweed	Royal Border; YN&Berwick, R Stephenson, 1850	
		NT 994531
Bletchley, Bucks.	Denbigh Hall; L&BR, R Stephenson, 1838	SP 866351
Calstock, Cornwall	Bere Alston & Calstock Lt. R., 1908	SX 433687
Calvine, Tayside	Inverness & Perth Jnct., Joseph Mitchell, 1863	
		NN 802656
Chirk, Powys/Shropshire	Shrewsbury & Chester R., H Robertson, 1848	
		SJ 288372
Connel Ferry, Highland	Callander & Oban R., J W Barry, 1903	NM 911343
Consett, Co. Durham	Hownes Gill; S&DR, Thomas Bouch, 1858	NZ 095490
Conwy, Gwynedd	Chester & Holyhead, R Stephenson, 18xx	SH 786776
Culloden, Highland	Highland R., Murdoch Patterson, 1898	NH 763450
Dent Head, N Yorkshire	Midland Railway, John Crossley, 1875	SD 779841
Darlington, Co. Durham	Skerne; Stockton & Darlington R., I Bonomi, 1825	
		NZ 289157
Earlestown, Merseyside	Sankey Viaduct, L&M, G Stephenson, 1830	SJ 568947
Forth Bridge, Fife/Lothians	Forth Bridge Co., J Fowler & B Baker, 1890	NT 136793
Glenfinnan, Inverness-shire	W. Highland R., Simpson & Wilson, 1901	NM 910813
Hanwell, London	Wharncliffe viaduct, GWR, I K Brunel, 1841	TQ 150804
Harringworth, Leics.	82 arch viaduct; Midland R., J Underwood, 1879	
		SP 914975
Killiecrankie, Tayside	Inverness & Perth Jct. R., Joseph Miller, 1863	
		NN 918623
Knaresborough, N Yorks.	York-Knaresborough, 1851	SE 347569
Knucklas, Powys	Central Wales R., 1864	SO 249742
Llanfair PG, Gwynedd	Britannia; Chester & Holyhead; R Stephenson, 1851	
		SH 541711
Leaderfoot, Borders	Berwickshire Railway, 1865	NT 575437
Maidenhead, Berkshire	Thames bridge; GWR, I K Brunel, 18xx	SU 901810

Meldon, Devon	All iron; L&SWR, W Galbraith & R Church, 1874	
		SX 565924
Montrose, Tayside	South Esk; Caledonian R., 1881	NO 709571
Newcastle-upon-Tyne	High Level Bridge Co., R Stephenson, 1849	NZ 252636
Penshaw, Tyne & Wear	Victoria bridge, Durham Jct. R, 1838	NZ 396575
Rainhill	Liverpool & Manchester R., G Stephenson, 1829	
		SJ 491914
Ribblehead, N Yorkshire	Midland R., John Crossley, 1875	SD 761795
Runcorn, Cheshire	L&NWR, William Baker, 1869	SJ 509835
Saltash, Devon/Cornwall	Royal Albert Bridge, Cornwall R., I K Brunel, 1859	
		SX 587435
Southall, London	Windmill Rd. triple bridge, GWR, 18xx	TQ143796
Shrewsbury, Shropshire	Belvidere bridge; S&B/SURC, William Baker	
		SJ 519 125
Tadcaster, N. Yorkshire	York & North Midlands, poss. G T Andrews, 1848	
		SE 484438
Tay Bridge, Tayside/Fife	North British R., W H & C Barlow, 1887	NO 391278
Todmordern, W Yorkshire	Gauxholme bridge, Manchester & Leeds R., 1841	
		SD 931229★
Urquhart, Grampian	Speymouth; Great N. of Scotland, P Barnett, 1886	
		NJ 345641
Welwyn Viaduct	Great Northern Railway, W & J Cubitt, 1850	
		TL 246150
Willington, Tyne & Wear	Newcastle & Nth. Shields R, J & B Green, 1839	
		NZ 316664
Windsor, Berkshire	Great Western Railway, I K Brunel, 1849	SU 961773
Wylam, Northblnd.	Scotswood, Newburn & Wylam R., W Laws, 1876	
		NZ 111643

Tunnels

Tunnels were the most expensive and dramatic engineering marvels of the railway era but for obvious reasons have left few surface remains. Well over 1,000 were built for standard gauge lines and many others for the narrow gauge and the early horse-drawn ones.

Blaenavon, Gwent	Pwll-ddu tramway tunnel, 1815	SO 249110
Box, Wiltshire	West portal of GWR tunnel, I K Brunel, 1841	
		ST 857695
Bramhope, W. Yorkshire	North portal, Leeds & Thirsk R., T Grainger, 1849	
		SE 256437
Clayton, West Sussex	N. portal, London & Brighton R, J Raistrick, 1841	
		TQ 299141

Dundee, Tayside	Law; South portal, Dundee & Newtyle R., 1831	
		NO 395311
Dinmore, Herefordshire	South portal, S&H, Henry Robertson, 1853	SO 510515
Dover, Kent	Shakespeare Cliff, east portal, SER, 1844	TR 308399
Glenfield, Leicestershire	Leicester & Swannington R, G Stephenson, 1832	
		SK 545065
Grosmont, North Yorkshire	Portal, Whitby & Pickering R., G Stephenson, 1836	
		NZ 829051
Lydden, Kent	Lydden tunnel, LC&DR, 1861	TR 262470
Kilsby, Northamptonshire	South portal, L&BR, R Stephenson, 1838	SP 578697
Otley, West Yorkshire	Memorial to workers killed in Bramhope tunnel	
		SE 202455
Primrose Hill, London	South portal, L&BR., R Stephenson, 1838	TQ 276843
Ramsgate, Kent	S. portal of LC&DR tunnel, 1863	TR 387650
Standedge, West Yorkshire	South portal, Huddersfield & Manchester R, 1849	
		SE 007082
Strood, Kent	North portal, Canal, conv. to rail for SER, 1845	
		TQ 717724
Woodhead, Derbys./S Yorks	S. portal, SA&MR, C Vignolles & J Locke, 1845	
		SK114 999

Stations

The number of stations open to traffic at the end of the twentieth century is dramatically different to that at the start of it, when there were well over 6,000. The variety of stations in terms of size and architecture is vast.

Early Stations

Birmingham Curzon Street	London & Birmingham R., Philip Hardwick, 1837	
		SP080871
Edge Hill, Liverpool	Liverpool & Manchester R., 1836	SJ 375900
Heighington, Co. Durham	Stockton & Darlington R., c.1830	NZ 272223
Manchester Liverpool Road	Liverpool & Manchester R., poss. T. Haigh, 1830	
		SJ 830978
Newtyle, Tayside	Dundee & Newtyle R., 1836	NO 299413
Watford 'old station', Herts.	London & Birmingham, G Aitchison, c.1837	
		TQ 107976

Major Town Stations

Bristol Temple Meads	GWR, I K Brunel, 1840; extended twice since	
		ST 608735
Cardiff Central	Great Western Railway, 1932-4	ST 182757
Carlisle Citadel	Caledonian/Lancaster & Carlisle Rs, W. Tite, 1847	
		NY 403553
Derby, Derbyshire	Midland R. and others, Francis Thompson, 1840	
		SK 363355
Edinburgh Waverley	North British R, rebuilt 1892-1902	
		NT 262738
Glasgow Central	Caledonian R., R Rowand Anderson *et al*, 1879 on	
		NS 587650
Glasgow Queen Street	North British R., James Carswell, 1877	NS 592653
Huddersfield, W. Yorkshire	Huddersfield & Manchester R., J P Pritchett, 1847	
		SE 143170
Liverpool Lime Street	L&NWR, W Baker and F Stevenson from 1867	
		SJ 352905
London King's Cross	Great Northern Railway, Lewis Cubitt, 1852	TQ 302830
London Liverpool Street	Great Eastern Railway, Edward Wilson, 1875	TQ 333818
London London Bridge	Rebuilt LB&SCR and SER, 1863	TQ 330802
London Paddington	GWR, I K Brunel & M Digby Wyatt, 1851-3	TQ 265814
London St. Pancras	MR, W H Barlow & G G Scott, 1868-76	TQ 301830
London Victoria	LC&DR & LB&SCR, 1860-2, rebuilt 1908	TQ 289789
London Waterloo	London & South Western R., J R SCott, 1922	
		TQ 311799
Manchester Central, GMC,	Cheshire Lines Cttee., poss. John Fowler, 1880	
		SJ 827977
Manchester Victoria, GMC	Lancashire & Yorkshire R., William Dawes, 1909	
		ST 833983
Newcastle-upon-Tyne, Tyns.	York, Newcastle & Berwick R., J Dobson, 1850	
		NZ 245638
Perth, Tayside	Caledonian, N. British, Highland Rs.; W Tite 1847	
		NO 114229
Stoke-on-Trent, Staffs	North Staffordshire R., attrib. H A Hunt, 1849	
		SJ 879455
Wolverhampton High Level	Queen St. entrance, S&BR, William Baker, 1849	
		SO 920985
Wolverhampton Low Level	OW&WR, attrib. partly to I K Brunel, 1854-5	
		SO 922989

Medium Sized Stations

Ashby-de-la-Zouch, Leics.	Midland Railway, 1849	SK 355163
Bath Green Park, Avon	Midland R., J H Sanders & J S Crossley, 1870	
		ST 745647
Bridgend, Mid-Glam	South Wales Railway, I K Brunel, 1850	SS 909798
Buxton, Derbys.	L&NWR, attrib. Jospeh Paxton, 1863	SK 058739
Cambridge	Eastern Counties R., Francis Thompson, 1845	
		TL 462573
Canterbury West, Kent	South Eastern R., Samuel Beazley, 1846	TR 145584
Carnforth, Lancs.	Lancaster & Carlisle R., William Tite, 1846	SD 496707
Chester, Cheshire	Joint C&H and S&C, Francis Thompson, 1848	
		SJ 414669
Cupar, Fife	Edinburgh & Northern R., 1847	
		NO 379143
Darlington North Road	Stockton & Darlington R., 1842	NZ 289156
Gravesend, Kent	South Eastern R., Samuel Beazley, 1849	TQ 647738
Hereford	Shrewsbury & Hereford R., R E Johnston, 1852-3	
		SO 516406
Inverness, Highland	Inverness & Nairn R., 1855 and later	NH 669456
Knighton, Powys	Knighton Railway, 1861	SO 294723
London Fenchurch Street	London & Blackwall, G. Berkeley, 1854	TQ 335809
London Marylebone	Great Central Railway	TQ 275821
Margate, Kent	Southern Railway, W Szlumper, 1926	TR 347705
Monkwearmouth, T&W	Brandling Junct. R., Thomas Moore, 1848	NZ 395577
Needham Market, Suffolk	Ipswich & Bury R., Frederick Barnes, 1846	TM 093546
North Woolwich	Eastern Counties R, attrib. Sancton Wood, 1847	
		TQ 431797
Penzance, Cornwall	West Cornwall R., I K Brunel, 1852; later changes	
		SW 479306
Shrewsbury, Shropshire	Joint, S&C, S&B, S&H, SURC; T Penson, 1848-9	
		SJ 494129
Stonehaven, Grampian	Aberdeen R., c.1849-50	NO 864861
Stroud, Gloucestershire	GWR, I K Brunel, 1845	SO 851051
Welshpool, Powys	Oswestry & Newtown R., 1860	SJ 229072
Windsor & Eton, Berks.	Riverside, L&SWR, William Tite, 1849	SU 969773
Worcester Shrub Hill	GWR, Edward Wilson, 1865	SO 857551

Country & Suburban Stations

Alton Towers, Staffs.	North StaffordshireR., attrib. Charles Barry, 1849
	SK 071427
Arley, Worcestershire	Severn Valley Railway, 1863 · SO 763799
Battle, East Sussex	South Eastern Railway, William Tress, 1852 · TQ 756154
Belford, Northumberland	Newcastle & Berwick R., Benjamin Green, 1847
	★NU 117349
Boat of Garten, Highland	Inverness & Perth Junction R., 1863; rebuilt 1904
	NH 943188
Brechin, Tayside	Aberdeen R., 1847; extended 1895 · NO 604601
Charlbury, Oxfordshire	OW&WR, a Brunel standard design, 1853 · SP 354192
Chepstow, Gwent	South Wales Railway, 1850 · ST 536936
Culham, Oxfordshire	Great Western R., a Brunel standard design, 1845
	SU 529953
Dingwall, Highland	Highland R., 1886 · NH 554584
Dunkeld, Tayside	Perth & Dunkeld R., Andrew Heiton, 1856 · NO 031415
Glasgow St Enoch	Glasgow District Subway Company, 1895 · NS 599650
Gleneagles, Tayside	Caledonian R., James Miller, 1919 · NN 929104
Hampton Court, London	L&SWR, William Tite, 1849 · TQ 154683
Hatch End, Great London	L&NWR, Gerald Horsley, 1911 · TQ 131914
Ladybank, Fife	Edinburgh & Northern R., attrib. David Bell, 1847
	NO 307096
Ridgmont, Bedfordshire	Bedfordshire R., 1846 · SP 965373
Rye, East Sussex	South Eastern R., William Tress, 1851 · TQ 919205
Sandon, Staffs.	North Staffordshire Railway, 1849 · SJ 947293
Surbiton, London	Southern Railway, 1937 · TQ 181673
Thurgarton, Notts.	Midland Railway, 1846 · SK 699485
Thurso, Highland	Sutherland & Caithness R., 1874 · ND 113675
Wemyss Bay, Strathclyde	Caledonian R., J Miller & D Mathieson, 1903
	NS 193685
Woburn Sands, Beds.	Bedfordshire R., 1846 · SP 923363
Wylam, Northumberland	Newcastle & Carlisle R., Benjamin Green, 1838
	NZ 120645

Miscellanea

Brownhills, W. Midlands	Canal aqueduct, S. Staffordshire R., 1856 · SK 053064
Carnforth, Lancs.	LMS Locomotive sheds, now Steamtown museum
	SD 496708
Chalk Farm, London	Roundhouse, L&BR, mainly R Stephenson, 1847
	TQ 282843
Crewe, Cheshire	Crewe Works and town, GJR then LNWR · SJ 710551

Derby, Derbyshire	Roundhouse, shed and works, Midland R., 1840 on	
		SK 366356
Ladybank, Fife	Workshops, Edinburgh & Northern R., c.1847	
		NO 307096
Seascale, Cumbria	Turreted water tower, Furness R., late-C19th?	
		NY 038011
Shrewsbury, Shropshire	Severn Bridge signal box, L&NWR, 1903	SJ 497126
Starcross, Devon	Pumping station, for Atmospheric R., Brunel, 1846	
		SX 977818
Stroud, Gloucestershire	Goods shed, GWR, 1845	SO 851051
Swindon, Wiltshire	GWR works and railway village, 1841 on	SU 141850
Wolverhampton, W Mids.	Goods shed, ex-S&CR, William Baker, c.1849	
		SO 922986
Wolverton, Bucks.	Carriage Works, L&NWR	SP 818413
Wymondham. Norfolk	Warehouse, Norfolk Railway, c.1845	TG 114008
York, Yorkshire	National Railway Museum, Leeman Road	SE 594519

Bibliography

There are literally hundreds of books published on railways and railway related subjects every year. Most are detailed and specific — usually the history of a particular line or the development of a certain class of locomotives. Many are general photographic albums, a large majority of which seem to be of the 1950s and 1960s. Very few books deal directly with the archaeology of the railways, though there are a small, but growing, number of studies on railway architecture. The following list is necessarily selective but includes most of the relevant standard texts; it excludes the many other books which also contain some useful information — such as the company histories, biographies of engineers, and material published prior to the 1960s.

Baxter, B, *Stone Blocks & Iron Rails* (1966)

Biddle, G, & Nock, O S, *The Railway Heritage of Britain* (1983)

Biddle, G, *Great Railway Stations of Britain* (1986)

Biddle, G, *The Railway Surveyors* (1990)

Binding, J, *Brunel's Cornish Viaducts* (1993)

Binney, M, & Pearce, D (eds.), *Railway Architecture* (1979)

Blower, A, *British Railway Tunnels* (1964)

Brooke, D, *The Railway Navvy* (1983)

Coleman, T, *The Railway Navvies* (1968)

Cope, G H (ed.), *British Railway Track* (1993)

Cossins, N, *The BP Book of Industrial Archaeology* (1987)

Croome, D F, & Jackson, A A, *Rails through the Clay* (1993)

Gilham, J C, *The Age of the Electric Train: Electric Trains in Britain since 1883* (1988)

Hadfield, C, *Atmospheric Railways* (1967)

Jackson, A A, *London Terminii* (1985)

James, L, *A Chronology of the Construction of Britain's Railway 1778-1855* (1983)

Jowett, A, *Jowett's Railway Atlas of Great Britain and Ireland* (1989)

Lewin, H G, *The Railway Mania and its Aftermath* (1968)

Lewis, M J T, *Early Wooden Railways* (1970)

Morgan, B, *Railways: Civil Engineering* (1971)

Mumms, R T, *Milk Churns to Merry-go-Round: A Century of Train Operation* (1986)

Nock, O S, *Railway Signalling* (1980)

Nock, O S (ed.), *Encyclopaedia of Railways* (1977)

Ottley, G, *Bibliography of British Railway History* (1983)

Ottley, G, *Supplement to the Bibliography of British Railway History* (1988)

Ransome, P J G, *The Archaeology of Railways* (1981)

Rhodes, M, *The Illustrated History of British Marshalling Yards* (1988)

Richards, J, & MacKenzie, J M, *The Railway Station: A Social History* (1986)

Robbins, M, *The Railway Age* (1962)

Signalling Study Group, *The Signal Box: A Pictorial history and Guide to Designs* (1986)

Simmons, J, *The Railway in Town and Country 1830-1914* (1986)

Simmons, J, *The Victorian Railway* (1991)

Simmons, J & Biddle, G, (eds.), *The Oxford Companion to British Railway History* (1997)

Smith, M, *British Railway Bridges & Viaducts* (1994)

Warn, C R, *Waggonways & Early Railways of Northumberland* (1976)

Wood, L V, *Bridges for Modellers* (1985)

Vanns, M A, *Signalling in the Age of Steam* (1995)

Index

Gauge Act, 28
George, Watkin, 86
Glasgow, Paisley, Kilmarnock & Ayr
    Railway, 59, 86
goods depots, 135-142, **136-141**
Grainger, Thomas, 106
Grand Junction Railway, 53, 56, 157
Great Central Railway, 31, 38, 78, 130,
    142
Great North of England Railway, 116
Great North of Scotland Railway, 78
Great Northern Railway, 52, 84, 89
Great Western Railway, 28, 31, 41, 44, 56,
    58, 70, 73, 76, 77, 82, 89, 99, 103,
    106, 114, 115, 120, 122, 123, 125,
    131, 135, 140, 144, 146, 149, 155,
    157, 161, 162, 172
Green, Benjamin, 78, 119
Green, John, 78
Green, Leslie, 130

Hannaford, J R, 123
Hawkshaw, John, 100, 106
Haytor Granite Tramway, 53
Highland Railway, 78, 84, 97
Hill, Thomas, 99
Holden, Charles, 131
Hudson, George, 26
hund, 18
Hunt, H A, 119

inclines, 23, 25, 26, 35, 37, 61, 62, **62**,
    64, 65, **64**, 66, 67, 171
Inverness, 84, **145**
Inverness & Perth Junction Railway, 73,
    84, 106
Inverness & Ross-shire Railway, 84

James, William, 22
Jessop, Josiah, 63
Jessop, William, 22, 48, 49, 80

Kennard, T W, 94
Ketley Canal, 50
Killingworth Colliery, 49
Kilmarnock & Troon Railway, 50, 80

Lancaster Canal, 23, 63
Landmann, Colonel G T, 82
Lawson Colliery, near Newcastle-on-
    Tyne, 49
Leeds & Thirsk Railway, 106
Leicester & Swannington Railway, 65,
    101
level crossings, 157-8, **158**
Little Eaton Tramway, 50
Liverpool, 100
Liverpool & Manchester Railway, 12, 18,
    22, 23, 25, 26, 37, 41, 43, 50, 53, 56,
    61, 62, 65, 66, 73, 81, 82, 100, 110,
    111, 113, 121, 122, 135, 136
Livock, J V, 106
Llanelli, **145**
Llangollen Railway Society, 18
Locke, Joseph, 53, 100, 104, 105, 125
locomotive depots, 143-9, **144-6**
London & Birmingham Railway, 37, 41,
    53, 65, 88, 102, 106, 112, 125, 136,
    144, 150, 157
London & Blackwall Railway, 56, 66
London & Brighton Railway, 56, 83, 106
London & Croydon Railway, 69, 151, 152
London & Greenwich Railway, 55, 82,
    151
London & North Eastern Railway, 31,
    161
London & North Western Railway, 55,
    60, 119, 140, 146, 155

Shropshire & Montgomeryshire Light
   Railway, 13
Shropshire Canal, 23, 62, 139
signal boxes, 151-5, **152-4**
Snailbeach District Railways, **141**
Stations:

   Alton Towers, 132; Bath Green
   Park, 132; Birmingham Curzon
   Street, **25**, 113, 136; Birmingham
   New Street, 126-7; Birmingham
   Snow Hill, 130, 132; Blackwall,
   66; Bristol Temple Meads, 10,
   122, 129, 135; Cambridge, 114;
   Canterbury, West, **114**; Cemmaes
   Road, **117**; Chalk Farm, **130**;
   Chester, 114; Crewe, 56, 116,
   118; Culham, 120; Darlington
   North Road, 110 Derby, 34, 114;
   Dundee, West, **31**; Edge Hill,
   111-2, **111**, 106; Edinburgh
   Waverley, 106, 116; Felling, 119;
   Frome, **121**, 123; Glasgow
   Central, 129; Glasgow, St.
   Enoch, 34, 129; Gobowen, 120;
   Haven Street, Isle of Wight, **32**;
   Heighington, 113; Huddersfield,
   121; Leamington Spa, 130;
   Liverpool Crown Street, 26, 37,
   65, 100, 110, 111, 113; Liverpool
   Lime Street, 65, 111, 125, 126,
   127; London Euston, 10, 15, 24,
   33, 37, 40, 65, 112-3, **112**, 116,
   122-3, 124, 125, 127, 144;
   London Fenchurch Street, 66;
   London King's Cross, **29**, 112,
   123-4, **122**, 127, 129, 139;
   London Liverpool Street, 129;
   London, London Bridge, 82, 112,
   124, 129, 155; London
   Marylebone, 130; London
   Minories, 66; London
   Paddington, 107, 108, 112, 116,
   123, 125-6, 146; London St.
   Pancras, 33, 109, **124**, **125**, 127,

129, 135, 139, 154; London
Waterloo, 70, 117; Manchester
Central, **126**, 129, 132;
Manchester Liverpool Road,
110-11, 113, 136; Manchester
Victoria, 111; Margate, **14**, **149**;
Mitcham, 119; Monkwearmouth,
121; Moreton-on-Lugg, 119;
New Hadley Halt, **133**;
Newcastle Central, **28**, 125;
Pontfadog, **132**; Rainhill, **23**, 25,
66, 73, 82; Reading, 114; Rednal,
120; Ridgmont, **116**, 129;
Rossett, 120; Sandon, 119; St.
John's Wood, **131**; Selby, 136;
Shrewsbury, 10, 116, 120;
Stockton St. John's Road, 110;
Stoke on Trent, 119; Stonehaven,
120; Stroud, 135; Thurso, 123;
Tintern, 132; Wick, 123;
Winchester, **115**; Windsor &
Eton Riverside, **129**;
Wolverhampton High Level, 15,
113, 120, 121, 140;
Wolverhampton Low Level, 15,
113, 114, 121, 140, **139**;
Worcester Shrub Hill,**128**;
Yatton, 120; York, Old station,
15, 34, 116, 136; York, New
station, **127**, 129

Steam engines, stationary, 23, 25-6, 37,
   62-7, 68-70
South Devon Railway, 42, 69, 70, 78
South Durham & Lancashire Union
   Railway, 94
South Eastern Railway, 42, 59, 100, 101
South Staffordshire Railway, 73
South Wales Railway, 24, 30, 34, 49, 50,
   58, 59, 76, 77, 86, 91, 99, 110
Southern Railway, 31
Stanhope & Tyne Railway, 65
Stephenson, George, 24, 25, 39-40, 49,
   50, 52, 64-6, 81, 87, 92, 100, 116